PROCLAMATION:

Aids for Interpreting the Lessons of the Church Year

PENTECOST 2

SERIES B

Eduard Riegert
and
Richard H. Hiers

FORTRESS PRESS   Philadelphia, Pennsylvania

Table of Contents

Library of Congress Catalog Card Number 74-24960

ISBN 0-8006-4077-2

4752F75   Printed in U.S.A   1-4077

General Preface

Proclamation: Aids for Interpreting the Lessons of the Church Year is a series of twenty-six books designed to help clergymen carry out their preaching ministry. It offers exegetical interpretations of the lessons for each Sunday and many of the festivals of the church year, plus homiletical ideas and insights.

The basic thrust of the series is ecumenical. In recent years the Episcopal church, the Roman Catholic church, the United Church of Christ, the Christian Church (Disciples of Christ), the United Methodist Church, the Lutheran and Presbyterian churches, and also the Consultation on Church Union have adopted lectionaries that are based on a common three-year system of lessons for the Sundays and festivals of the church year. *Proclamation* grows out of this development, and authors have been chosen from all of these traditions. Some of the contributors are parish pastors; others are teachers, both of biblical interpretation and of homiletics. Ecumenical interchange has been encouraged by putting two persons from different traditions to work on a single volume, one with the primary responsibility for exegesis and the other for homiletical interpretation.

Despite the high percentage of agreement among the traditions, both in the festivals that are celebrated and the lessons that are appointed to be read on a given day, there are still areas of divergence. Frequently the authors of individual volumes have tried to take into account the various textual traditions, but in some cases this has proved to be impossible; in such cases we have felt constrained to limit the material to the Lutheran readings.

The preacher who is looking for "canned sermons" in these books will be disappointed. These books are one step removed from the pulpit: they explain what the lessons are saying and suggest ways of relating this biblical message to the contemporary situation. As such they are springboards for creative thought as well as for faithful proclamation of the word.

The authors of this volume of *Proclamation* are Eduard R. Riegert and Richard H. Hiers. Dr. Riegert, the editor-homiletician, is a graduate of the University of Saskatchewan (B.A.), the Lutheran College and Seminary in Saskatoon (B.D.), the Lutheran Theoolgical Seminary in Philadelphia (S.T.M.), and Princeton Theological Seminary (Ph.D.). He has been teaching at Waterloo Lutheran Seminary, Waterloo, Ontario, since 1965 and is currently Associate Professor of Homiletics and Liturgics and Dean of the Chapel. In addition, he is also Lecturer in Archaeology,

Wilfrid Laurier University, Waterloo, Ontario. Dr. Riegert is an ordained Lutheran minister and a member of the Lutheran Church in America. Dr. Hiers, the exegete, is a graduate of Yale Divinity School (B.D.), with a major in New Testament, and Yale University (Ph.D.), with a major in biblical theology. He is Professor of Religion, University of Florida, Gainesville. He is a member of the Protestant Episcopal Church and an ordained minister in the Presbyterian Church, U.S.

Introduction

One of the intimidating and yet liberating lessons the preacher must learn is that he becomes an interpreter of Scripture. Nowhere is this lesson better learned than in close dialogue with a biblical scholar. This volume, like others in this series, invites the reader to join the dialogue a preacher and a biblical scholar have had.

We have offered exegesis (thought not exposition) of all the denominationally appointed texts, and wish to record our impression that remarkable insight has gone into the selection of these combinations of lessons by the several traditions, especially with respect to the related and ultimate issues they coherently embrace. We have not, however, attempted to smooth out all differences in interpretation between us. Both the Scriptures and human life are too rich for a "party line" approach. Occasionally one or the other of us does take a fairly definite theological and/or ethical position or follow a different perspective or interest; but we think we ought to do so, for the preacher must do so, too.

It is only fair, furthermore, to acknowledge that we assume, necessarily, a series of critical and historical positions which, given the limits of our assignment, we cannot explicate or even define adequately; nevertheless, we have endeavored to avoid premature cloture with respect to traditional interpretations as well as to the latest conclusions in biblical research (e.g., the authorship of Ephesians; the historical value of the Markan tradition). Our assumption is that the reader will have access to major commentaries, monographs, and journals. For this reason, too, as well as because of limitations of space, we have not provided footnotes to scholarly literature.

The homiletical expositions were born out of independent study of and meditation upon the texts, and subsequently shaped by direct confrontation with the exegetical studies. Their intent is not so much to provide clusters of sermon ideas as to move imaginatively into the realm of human life as this is suggested, challenged, and illuminated by the text. A basic principle underlying the expositions is that kerygmatically and experientially the story of the text is our story. Historically Joshua and Jeremiah and even Jesus are far removed from us, but their struggles with faith and life are not. Any good story grips us and takes us into it, so that we identify with the characters and the situations; thus it articulates at least some of our experiences and problems. The Bible does this too. Thus, the shift from Jeremiah, for example, to ourselves occurs in a split second: we *are* Jeremiah complaining to the Lord. And through this imaginative process we gain meaning for ourselves, and through faithful exegesis we find also correction.

While it may be obvious, it is nevertheless well to set forth the reminder that the exegetical studies themselves are prime material for sermons. The wide range of biblical references given (to mention only one facet) forms a reservoir of material for "expository" sermons which teach the Scriptures, and for "doctrinal" sermons which treat theological themes. It goes without saying that neither the exegesis nor the exposition will make sense to the reader unless he has before him and carefully attends to the biblical text.

We wish to acknowledge the use of the Revised Standard Version in most direct quotations, as well as Kittel's and Nestle's texts.

E.R.R.
R.H.H.

The Tenth Sunday after Pentecost

Lutheran	Roman Catholic	Episcopal	Pres./UCC/Chr.	Methodist/COCU
Exod. 24:3-11	2 Kings 4:42-44	2 Kings 4:42-44	2 Kings 4:42-44	2 Kings 4:42-44
Eph. 4:1-7,	Eph. 4:1-6	Eph. 4:1-6	Eph. 4:1-6,	Eph. 4:1-6,
11-16			11-16	11-16
John 6:1-15	John 6:1-15	Mark 6:35-44	John 6:1-15	John 6:1-15

EXEGESIS

First Lesson: Exod. 24:3-11 (and 2 Kings 4:42-44). Exodus 20-23 reports the various "words" and ordinances which, according to the tradition, God spoke to Moses on Mt. Sinai as the law for Israel. Because of the holiness of God, the people had to keep their distance from God, but Moses had drawn near to him (20:21). Our lesson describes what follows, when Moses comes down and tells the people what God has said. Immediately and unanimously they declare their intention to keep the law (24:3). [In later times, the elders of Israel enacted a more elaborate ceremony of ratification or renewal of the covenant. See Deuteronomy 27-30.] Afterwards, Moses "wrote all the words of the Lord," thereby producing "the book of the Covenant" (24:7) which, presumably, contained both the Ten Commandments (20:1-17) and the numerous other laws recorded in 20:23-23:33. Moses then built an altar at the foot of Mt. Sinai, erected twelve pillars, representing the tribes of Israel, and ordered sacrificial offerings. The blood of the animals was drained off, in accordance with the ancient belief that it was their life (Gen. 9:4-5). Having thrown half the blood against the altar, Moses then read the "book of the Covenant" to the people, who again vowed fidelity to it (v. 7). Then he threw the rest of the blood upon the people, symbolizing, perhaps, the sacred bond of unity or community between God and people. Nadab and Abihu were sons of Aaron, according to later priestly belief (Exod. 6:23; Num. 3:2 ff.). They, together with Moses, Aaron, and seventy (other) elders then went back up Mt. Sinai and "saw the God of Israel"—an unusual episode, since God was only rarely *seen* (Isa. 6:1 ff.; Ezek. 1:26-28; cf. Exod. 3:3-6). God is not described, but only that on which he stood: "as it were, a pavement of sapphire stone," through which translucent surface, perhaps, he was visible. God did not come into direct contact with the men, but they were allowed to see him and to eat and drink in his presence (v. 11). Possibly it was thought that Moses and the others were given a share of the sacrificial offerings, though what they ate and drank is not stated. The meal, like the sprin-

1

kling with blood, indicated communion with God. Later Jewish traditions looked forward to eating and drinking in the presence of God or his messiah in the kingdom of God (Isa. 25:6; 2 *Baruch* 29; cf. Gen. 49:10–12).

2 Kings 4:42–44. A man brings Elisha a supply of "bread of the first fruits" (see Exod. 23:16), namely, twenty barley loaves and a sack of grain. This may have been a typical offering to the priests or prophets who presided at the cultic altars in those days. Elisha orders his servant to set this before "the men," i.e., the group of cultic prophets mentioned in 2 Kings 4:38. The servant protests that this will not be enough for a hundred men. Elisha insists. The servant then did as directed, the men ate, and there was some left. The story was told, with others in 2 Kings 2–7, to commemorate Elisha's not always beneficent miraculous powers (see 2:23 f.), and to show that God could take care of those in special need (4:1–41). It is noteworthy that few such miracle stories are reported in the OT, and that most of them are associated with Elisha.

Second Lesson: Eph. 4:1–7, 11–16. We come now to a series of five lessons (Pentecost 10–14) from chaps. 4 and 5 of the Epistle to the Ephesians. The words "who are at Ephesus" (1:1) are absent in the earliest manuscripts, suggesting either that this was a general or "catholic" letter for reading by several churches, or that it was intended for some church whose identity was undesignated or lost. There is little in the letter to suggest that the author was personally acquainted with its intended recipients (cf. Acts 19), and several hints that he had not been with them before, e.g., 1:15; 3:1–4. Of course, the letter might have been written before Paul first came to Ephesus. But there are other reasons to question whether Paul was its author. References to the apostles in 2:20 and 3:5 imply composition in the post-apostolic age. Numerous words are used here that are not found elsewhere in Paul's letters, and there are other stylistic differences. The letter parallels or reproduces a great deal of the distinctive content of Colossians, whose authorship also is disputed. Nevertheless, much of the faith-understanding in the letter is basically Pauline. Edgar Goodspeed and John Knox have proposed that it was written around A.D. 90 as a compend of Paul's thought and an introduction to a collection of Paul's letters then being assembled for copying and wider circulation among the churches. The main concerns of the letter are to appeal to readers to maintain the unity of the church, faithfulness to Christ, and renewed moral life befitting those who have been saved, brought near, called, or forgiven.

Here as elsewhere in Paul's letters, the author refers to himself as a "prisoner" (e.g., Phil. 1:7, 13; Philem. 23). Paul had been imprisoned on several occasions, including the final years of his career (Acts 21–28). The understanding of the Christian life in 4:1–3 is typical of the Pauline "indicative/imperative" (Bultmann). In effect: Strive to be what already, through the grace (gift) of God in Christ, you have become. There are a number of echoes of Paul's exhortations in 1 Corinthians 12–14 here: The summons to lowliness, meekness, patience, forbearance, and love (1 Cor. 13:4–7); to unity in the one Spirit (1 Cor. 12:4–13); and to peace and honoring all members of the community as members of the one body of Christ (1 Cor. 12:14–31). In Eph. 4:11 the different offices of the church are described as "gifts"; cf. 1 Cor. 12:4 ff., 27 ff. But in both, the final mark of the Christian life is love, doing that which contributes to building up the church (1 Cor. 13:13; 14:12; Eph. 4:12, 16). A special feature in Ephesians is the idea of growing or maturing into the stature or person of Christ: 4:13, 15–16. The emphasis in Ephesians is less on the future coming of Christ than on the transformation or confirmation of Christians by Christ to the measure of his perfection (see also 1:22; 2:16–19, and esp. 4:13). Paul's "Christ-mysticism" was similar in some respects, though Paul looked for final perfection, transformation or fulfillment only at the resurrection of the dead and the coming of Christ (1 Cor. 13:8–12; 15:42–55; Phil. 3:8–21).

Gospel: John 6:1–15; Mark 6:35–44. The Fourth Gospel generally presents a quite different account of Jesus, his message and activity, from that given in the first three (synoptic) Gospels. To what extent John contains historically reliable tradition beyond what we find in the synoptic Gospels is still debated. In any case, this Gospel represents the faith-understanding or theology of an important segment of the late first century Christian community. In our lesson today, we have John's version of Jesus' feeding of the five thousand. It is not very different from that given in Mark 6:32–44. John locates the meal "in the hills" (cf. Mark 6:46); omits reference to Jesus' compassion on the crowd and teaching (Mark 6:34); places the event near or at Passover (6:4); reports that Jesus knew what he would do and deliberately tested Philip by asking him how they would buy bread (cf. Mark 6:37); and that a lad, rather than the disciples, supplied barley loaves (cf. 2 Kings 4:42) and fish. In other respects, the stories are quite similar, including such details as two hundred denarii, five loaves, two fish, five thousand participants sitting on the grass, and twelve baskets of fragments left over.

In both versions, Jesus' procedure parallels or anticipates his actions at the last supper and the church's later reenactment of that event: the people are seated, Jesus takes bread, blesses or gives thanks, distributes to the crowd, likewise the fish (cf. cup). In Mark 6, Jesus also breaks the bread and distributes it through the disciples. If the procedure is already eucharistic in Mark, it is still more so in John. Such key terms as *anapesein, anakeimenois* (sit down), *elaben* (take), *eucharistēsas* (give thanks), and *edoken* (give), lacking in Mark but used by John, parallel and probably derive from the synoptic and Paul's accounts of the last supper

(Matthew 26, Mark 14, Luke 22, 1 Corinthians 11). In John, the story of the feeding of the five thousand seems to function as the "institution" of the eucharist, since John does not describe any such procedures at the last supper (chap. 13). As we shall see in the next three lessons, in the later verses of chap. 6 Jesus discourses about the bread which gives eternal life, identified with himself or his flesh, in what are, evidently, a series of eucharistic sayings (6:26–58). John may have intended the reader to understand that the bread about which Jesus spoke here was related to the ceremony involving bread and fish reported in the earlier verses of chap. 6.

Only John's Gospel describes any of Jesus' actions as "signs"; in this Gospel, signs are reported for the benefit of the reader: "that you may believe that Jesus is the Christ, the Son of God, and that believing you may have life in his name" (20:30–31). Thus the signs themselves have a kind of sacramental or saving value. But the people mentioned in 6:14–15 misread the sign: they identified Jesus as "the prophet who is to come" (a "prophet like Moses," Elijah, or Elisha?). And they desired to "snatch" or "seize" (*harpazein*: cf. Matt. 11:12; 12:29; 13:19; John 10:12) him and make him king. But this was not the kingship Jesus sought: My kingdom (or kingship) is not of (or from) this world (John 18:36; cf. Matt. 4:8–9).

HOMILETICAL INTERPRETATION

First Lesson: Exod. 24:3–11. Exotic narratives: on the one hand a "primitive" (barbaric? savage?) scene of covenant-making and covenant-ratification; on the other hand a sublime theophany and a feasting with God!

But the covenant has to do with life (the blood is the life), and life is messy . . . and sublime! The covenant is made here in the midst of life—in the midst of slavery-freedom, sin-grace, the blood of violence and the blood of brotherhood. We are all in that together even as all Israel was sprinkled with blood, and we are all "washed in the blood of the Lamb" and receive "the blood of Christ shed for you" (note the movement in John 6, covered progressively over the next several Sundays). We cannot escape this solidarity of mankind—nor should we want to; we are all inextricably bound to one another (note "one body, one Spirit . . ." in the Second Lesson, Ephesians 4); to be bound to one another is life; to be separated is death (quite dramatically so in our "spaceship earth" and our "global village").

If life is messy, it is also sublime. The covenant is from God and with God—already here in our messy and frequently dehumanizing life-together we catch glimpses of his presence. There is enormous commitment on the part of God; already he "humbles himself" to become part of our oft barbaric human existence, showing us in the midst of it the magnificent dimensions of life: the mountain of splendor, the vision of clarity, the feast of united celebration. All biblical feasts have that ultimate dimension: they are "foretastes" (see exegesis, v. 11).

Second Lesson: Eph. 4:1–7, 11–16.   There is much here that is instructive for the peculiarly Christian community. The churches (as do other institutions and groups) too often exaggerate their *differences* in order to justify their existence; Paul admonishes us to exercise watchful care over the *unity* which is already given through our calling. It is the unity of one body activated by one Spirit and motivated by one hope; it is made possible by one Lord with whom we are all united by one baptism which demonstrates and expresses one faith; it is a unity under one Father-God who permeates all (4:4–6). This unity is fragile; to care for it requires worthy living (4:1–3), which in turn produces worthy results: a mutual nurture leading to full maturity as measured in Christ (4:7, 11–16).

This unity held in the bond of peace recalls the ancient covenant with God (First Lesson). That covenant is here neither negated nor superseded, but expanded to its fullness: Gentiles are included in it (cf. Eph. 2:11 ff.)! This is a magnificent vision, an expansion of the ancient covenant which the writer calls a "mystery" (Eph. 3:3–6, 9–10). Over the centuries that ancient covenant became narrow and exclusivistic—that is a danger the people of the "new covenant" in later times, unfortunately, have not escaped! The writer to the Ephesians wrote from an *inclusive* perspective; the church's perspective on Jews and other non-Christians has been largely *exclusivistic*. Fragmentariness is a mark of our lives and of the world. Paul's vision of one body with distinct yet integrated members is not only a model for congregations but also for the community of nations.

Gospel: John 6:1–15.   The whole of John 6, with a few omissions, is read over the next five Sundays, Pentecost 10 through 14. We need therefore to grasp the movement of the entire chapter. One may see the thought moving on three levels: (1) the purely materialistic level in which hungry folk receive bread; (2) the still materialistic but advanced level in which bread signifies Jesus' flesh; (3) the illuminating level of the Spirit. Again, one may see a progression in a series of questions and answers, initiated by Jesus and concluded by Jesus:

6:5—How feed the people?	6:9—We can't. Can you?
6:25—When did you come here?	6:26 f.—Labor for the food of eternal life.
6:28—How do the work of God?	6:29—Believe in the one he sent.
6:30 f.—What sign do you do?	6:32 f.—God gives the bread of life.
6:34—Give us this bread.	6:35 ff.—I am the bread.
6:41 f.—How can he say he came down from Heaven?	6:43–51—I am the living bread=my flesh.

6:52—How can he give us his flesh to eat?

6:53-58—Mutual abiding.

6:60—Who can listen to this hard saying?

6:61-65—The spirit gives life.

6:66 f.—Will you also go away?

6:68 f.—You are the Holy One of Israel.

In today's Gospel Jesus initiates the discussion by feeding the 5,000. It is a "sign," says the evangelist, and this should alert us that interesting and even profitable themes like Jesus' compassion which triumphs over his weariness, Andrew still bringing people to Jesus, the boy and his lunch, the "facts and figures" Philip, and the abundant leftovers are definitely secondary themes. As a "sign" the miracle reaches *back*: back to Elisha's feeding miracle (2 Kings 4:42-44; Elisha is the carrier of Elijah's mantle, and Elijah was very important in Jewish messianic expectations); back to the feast with God of Moses and the 70 elders (First Lesson); to the Passover (6:4) and its themes of exodus and wilderness wanderings; and to Deut. 18:15, the "prophet who is to come" (6:14). As a "sign" the miracle also points *forward* to the advent of a New Age when God intervenes to save his people; to the cross and resurrection; to the eucharist; and to the eschatological banquet.

The "sign," discernible only to the eyes of faith, sets Jesus at the center of history as the one who makes clear God's constant and saving presence. The same God who led Israel out of Egypt, who fed them in the desert, who sustained them through centuries of convoluted history, is savingly present—incarnate—in this Jesus whose life is the life of the world, and remains savingly present in the eucharist, and indeed, into the ultimate future.

The Eleventh Sunday after Pentecost

Lutheran	Roman Catholic	Episcopal	Pres./UCC/Chr.	Methodist/COCU
Exod. 16:2-15	Exod. 16:2-4, 12-15	Exod. 16:2-4, 12-15	Exod. 16:2-4, 12-15	Exod. 16:2-15
Eph. 4:17-24	Eph. 4:17, 20-24	Eph. 4:17-24	Eph. 4:17-24	Eph. 4:17-25
John 6:24-35	John 6:24-35	John 6:24-35	John 6:24-35	John 6:24-35

EXEGESIS

First Lesson: Exod. 16:2-15. The story picks up here immediately after the escape from Pharaoh's armies by the Red Sea (Sea of Reeds) celebrated in the songs of Miriam and Moses, chap. 15. Moses had purified the "bitter" water of Marah, and the people, having encamped at the oasis of Elim (15:27), now come into the Wilderness of Sin (= Zin, Sinai?). It is still only a few weeks after their deliverance by the sea (16:1), but already the people complain against Moses and Aaron, that it would have been better if they had never left Egypt with its ample supply of meat ("fleshpots") and bread. In their anxiety and discomfort, they profoundly mistrust Moses' intentions or ability: "You have brought us out into this wilderness to kill this whole assembly with hunger" (v. 3). Moses correctly perceives that their "murmurings" are not so much against himself and Aaron, as against the Lord (vv. 7–8).

The "murmuring" or complaining of the people of Israel in the wilderness is a characteristic feature of the biblical reports concerning this period. (Thus also, e.g., Numbers 11, 14 and Exodus 32, which give mainly J and E traditions.) Probably we have here a P (Priestly) account: Note the prominence of Aaron, provision for obviating the necessity of gathering (doing labor) on the Sabbath (v. 5), and the typically P description of God's visible presence in terms of his "glory" (*kabōd*), vv. 7, 10. Only a few days after the exodus events, the people are again (cf. 14:11–12) doubting whether the Lord cares or is able to sustain them. They do not pray, but only complain. Nevertheless, the Lord hears their "murmurings" and undertakes to provide for them. So quails "came up and covered the camp," supplying flesh or meat (*basar*), and in the morning "there was on the face of the wilderness" a peculiar substance, identified, perhaps, as manna (*man*), and as bread (*lechem*). Thus God provided the flesh and bread for want of which they had complained (v. 3). What the "manna" may have been was a mystery then (v. 15), and has remained so since, though interpreters have offered many more or less naturalistic explanations. It is described as a "fine, flake-like thing, fine as hoarfrost on the ground," and also "like coriander seed" (vv. 14, 31). The term *lechem* may mean simply "food" as well as "bread"; we should not visualize loaves of bread, though this is suggested in later times, e.g., John 6:31. In any case, here, as in the great exodus event, God showed himself willing and able to care for his people. Later in the chapter, it is said that the people continued to eat manna all their years in the wilderness until they came to the land of Canaan (v. 35).

It is remarkable that these reports of Israel's complaining and mistrust are found in their Scriptures. Yet it is typical of the faith and historical traditions of Israel that the faults of the people are openly reported. Jacob, David, Solomon, and even Abraham and Moses, are shown in their moments of disbelief, disobedience, and—in the case of Solomon—apostasy. There are heroes, but no saints in the OT. The basic distinction between God and people central to Israel's faith permitted the story of Israel to be told realistically, with surprisingly little self-glorification (cf. Ezra 9:2). The sermons in the early chapters of Deuteronomy continually

emphasize that it was not because of Israel's importance or virtue that
God made covenant with them and blessed them, but because of his
promise to the fathers and his love for them (e.g., Deut. 7:6–8; 9:4–6).
We see here already the understanding that God's favor and blessings
flow from his love or grace, not because of man's—even Israel's—righteousness (cf. Rom. 3:20–26; 1 Cor. 1:26–31).

Second Lesson: Eph. 4:17–24. Paul (or the Pauline author) exhorts
the readers to live the kind of life befitting the new humanity which has
been made possible for them. Vv. 17–19 contrast the life that Christians
must live with that of the Gentiles; vv. 20–21 refer to the standard of
Christ which they should have learned; and vv. 22–24 call upon the
readers to put off their old nature (literally, "old man") with its corrupt
ways of life, and put on the new one of true righteousness and holiness.

Paul does not usually speak disparagingly of the Gentiles: they were,
in fact, the subjects of his special theological concern and missionary activity (Gal. 1–3). Eph. 4:17–19 echoes Paul's description in Rom. 1:18–32
of those, presumably Gentiles, who failed to perceive the "power and
deity" of God in the world, who "became futile in their thinking and their
senseless minds were darkened," and consequently were given up to
"dishonorable passions" and all kinds of improper conduct. Increasingly
the churches of the latter part of the first century were composed of
Gentile-Christians, who had not been brought up in accordance with the
law and customs of Jewish morality. If Ephesians was written to such
a church (or churches), its summons to live differently from the ways of
the Gentile neighbors and from the readers' own former Gentile patterns
of behavior, would be very much to the point. Thus, probably, Eph.
4:22; cf. 1 Cor. 6:9–11.

The expressions "learning Christ," "hearing about him," and being
"taught in him" (vv. 20–21) are unusual. Paul only infrequently refers to
traditions about Jesus or his teaching. Here, however, the sense may be
more the mystical participation of the believer in Christ, an immediate
perception of his being and will, as in Phil. 2:5: "Have this mind among
yourselves, which you have in Christ Jesus . . ." Here the author calls
on his readers to be renewed in the spirit of their minds (Eph. 4:23).

Paul's insistence that those in Christ are already a "new creation"
(*kainē ktisis:* see 2 Cor. 5:17; Gal. 6:15) is presupposed in the summons
to put off the old man and put on the new (*ton kainon anthrōpon*),
"created [*ktisthenta*] after the likeness of God" (4:22–24). A quite
similar saying is to be found at Col. 3:9–10, again contrasting the "old
man" with the "new," but with the slight difference that the latter is
indicative rather than hortatory, and it is a matter of *"being renewed in
knowledge* after the image of its creator." Cf. 1 Cor. 15:49: "Just as we
have borne the image of the man of dust, we shall [or "let us"] bear
the image of the man of heaven." Paul normally thinks of the believer's

being conformed or transformed to the image of Christ, rather than to the likeness of God. On being like God in righteousness and holiness, see, e.g., Lev. 19:2 ff.; Matt. 5:48. The idea that the Christian already is, or should be transformed is basic both to Paul and—if not the same person—the author of Ephesians (see also Rom. 12:1-2).

Gospel: John 6:24–35. After feeding the five thousand, Jesus and also his disciples crossed the Sea of Galilee to Capernaum. Jesus walked the first part of the way on water, rather than traveling by boat with his disciples, to the temporary mystification of the people who had not seen him leave by boat and so looked for him the next morning in the vicinity of the meal of bread and fish (6:16-24). Afterwards they find him at Capernaum. Despite what seem to be several non sequiturs in the dialogue that follows between Jesus and "the people" (later identified as "the Jews," vv. 41, 52), there are a number of related contrasts and associations of terms and concepts.

The people address Jesus as "rabbi" or teacher (v. 25), but he refers to himself as "Son of man" (v. 27), a title with divine connotation in John. They ask him when he came there (v. 25). But Jesus ignores this, and tells them that they do not seek him because they saw signs (presumably this refers to the feeding of the five thousand the day before, John 6:14), but they seek him, he says, because they ate their fill of loaves (v. 26), as if they were simply interested in another free or filling meal. (The expression, "you ate your fill" is reminiscent of the feeding of Israel in the wilderness from the First Lesson: Exod. 16:8, 12, 16. This is referred to explicitly in John 6:31-33 where the expressions "bread from heaven" and "bread which comes down from heaven" probably allude to Exod. 16:4. See also Ps. 78:23-24.) Jesus admonishes them not to seek such food, but to seek the food or true bread from heaven which endures to and gives eternal life (vv. 27, 33, 35). As in the eucharistic-soteriological sayings that follow (esp. vv. 48-58), the Johannine Jesus identifies this food or bread with himself. It is he who has "come down from heaven" (6:38, 50-51).

Strangely, they reply, "What must we do, to be doing the work (*ergon*) of God?" (v. 28). Perhaps the connection is by verbal association with Jesus' statement in v. 27, "Do not labor" (or "work," *ergazesthe*). Or it may be that the evangelist intended to contrast Jewish emphasis on doing the works of the law with believing in Jesus. At any rate, the work of God they should do, Jesus tells them, is to believe in him (v. 29). Then they do ask for a "sign" or demonstration as basis for believing him (v. 30), but not, significantly, for believing *in* (*eis*) him (cf. vv. 29, 35).

It is not certain whether these sayings really refer to the eucharistic bread. In this lesson, Jesus does not call on the people to eat (or drink), but to *believe in* him. This is the "work of God" that they must do (v. 29). He who comes to Jesus and believes in him will not hunger or thirst (v. 35). Jesus is bread, then, in the spiritual or symbolic sense that those who believe in him receive the "food" or "bread" of life, eternal life (vv. 27, 33, 35, 40).

HOMILETICAL INTERPRETATION

First Lesson: Exod. 16:2–15. Moses is angry! It is no small thing to be accused of leading a people into the wilderness to perish—and that they might do so may well have crossed his own mind more than once. Besides, "murmuring" is at once irritating and infectious. To be reminded of "how things used to be"—before all these precipitous changes occurred —makes one's teeth grate, especially if one is the initiator of change and has no more than a future hope to set forth as justification. Yet how can the people of Abraham (and of Jesus!) keep forgetting the promise, and keep mislaying their commitment to the covenant (see Pentecost 10, First Lesson)? It is hard to shake a slavish mentality, to put off the old and put on the new (Second Lesson), to venture from the known—no matter how dreary it is—into the unknown. Yet that is our human journey.

While Moses is angry, God, against whom the murmuring is ultimately directed, is magnificently lenient: "I will rain bread from heaven . . ."! But not vapidly lenient: "that I may prove them, whether they will walk in my law or not." God's grace is also a judgment! He sets before us "exodus" opportunities, and our immediate reaction is one of shrinking back. Yet it is precisely *in* the opportunity that his sustaining grace can be discovered. The wilderness is a sore place that calls for "dying," and for those with the courage (or the desperation!) to die, it leads to the promised land of a new beginning and a new status. Miraculously, unexpected resources do appear.

Second Lesson: Eph. 4:17–24. Any convert, whether to or from a religion, an ideology, even an opinion, can grasp the dynamic of transformation detailed in this pericope. A conversion is a terrible invigoration! It is terrible because it means forsaking the familiar "old" for the strange "new," and that is a wrenching experience, full of pain, loss, sorrow, anguish. It is also invigorating, for it is fresh air, elbow room, excitement, adventure. It is like that moment when, having let go of one trapeze bar while reaching for the other, you hang suspended in sheer terror and sheer ecstasy. The people of the ancient exodus from Egypt knew it (see the First Lesson); so did Paul on the Damascus Road, Marx in the British Museum, and indeed, if we reflect on our progress in thought and life, we will find a variety of "conversions" we have experienced and/or backed away from.

We ought then to beware of reducing the transformation described in this pericope to a series of moralistic changes. Although ethics are definitely involved (v. 19), the writer is talking about a shift from one "manner of life" to another, from one stance or posture to another, from one "nature" to another, from being "in sin" to being "in grace." Unlike the shift made by the trapeze artist, this transformation does not occur in the twinkling of an eye (though the decision to change may so occur), but is a process that needs helping along—even with pointed reminders, 4:20–21. (Notice the progress toward understanding in John 6.) If we take our theological and experiential understanding of ourselves seriously *(simul justus et peccator)* we will glimpse something of the depth and length of this transformation, and its increasing radicalness: "after the likeness of God."

Gospel: John 6:24–35. It is amazingly difficult to rise above a sheerly physical and materialistic level of life (see under Pentecost 10, John 6:1–15). We are overwhelmingly preoccupied with survival ("the food which perishes"), yet vaguely hungering. As we struggle hard for the food which perishes, so we think we must also struggle hard for "the food which endures to eternal life"—unless there is a short-cut: "give us this bread always"!

Somewhere at the root of it is our self-understanding and our subsequent God-understanding. We are "nature's man," and like every other creature strive to survive today and tomorrow, and any windfall extends survival to the day after tomorrow. We are "manipulative man" who, if he does the right thing (pushes the right button, knows the right people, obeys the right rules, "operates" adroitly) will get an instant reward (like Moses in the wilderness). We are "absurd man," valiantly or resignedly going the weary round, pathetically hoping for a delivering miracle, yet suspicious of any promise ("What sign will you do?").

Is there something more? That's the sometimes sluggish, sometimes poignant question. Is there deliverance: a diamond ring in a box of antique junk? a winning lottery ticket? perhaps a wonder-working God?

Open your eyes and see! Deliverance is *here* (even as Jesus stands there before them, saying, "Believe in me"). We don't see it because we ask the wrong questions—penultimate questions related to our survival and to the immediate problematic situation. Are we (can we stretch that far?) "God's man"? If so, then "nature's man" is also a decision-maker; "manipulative man" is also a creator; "absurd man" is also transcendent. Man, like bread, can be only a chemical mixture, pummelled and subjected to enormous stress . . . or, like bread, he can be a medium of life, a sacrament, a means of grace.

How? That's the wrong question. Can I, like the grain of wheat in the earth and the loaf on the plate, die and thus bring life? Can I subsume my history into a greater history so that my history becomes part of God's history?

The Twelfth Sunday after Pentecost

Lutheran	Roman Catholic	Episcopal	Pres./UCC/Chr.	Methodist/COCU
1 Kings 19:4–8	1 Kings 19:4–8	1 Kings 19:4–8	1 Kings 19:4–8	1 Kings 19:4–8
Eph. 4:30–5:2	Eph. 4:30–5:2	Eph. 4:30–5:2	Eph. 4:30–5:2	Eph. 4:30–5:2
John 6:41–51	John 6:41–52	John 6:41–51	John 6:41–51	John 6:41–52

EXEGESIS

First Lesson: 1 Kings 19:4–8. Elijah, the great ninth century prophet in Israel, has just been vindicated in his contest with the prophets of Baal and Asherah on Mt. Carmel—that scene dramatized so memorably in Mendelssohn's "Elijah." Baal did not answer the cries of his prophets, but the Lord brought fire upon the offering Elijah had prepared. Then, at Elijah's command, the prophets of Baal were killed and, strangely obedient to Elijah's direction, the mighty but malevolent King Ahab meekly returned to his palace at Jezreel and his Phoenician wife, Jezebel (chap. 18). She was no believer in the Lord, and vowed vengeance upon Elijah by her pagan gods (19:1–2). He had humiliated, then (presumably) killed the four hundred prophets of Asherah who once sat at her table (18:19). Asherah probably was a female Canaanite deity. Jezebel regarded her own royal power as absolute; she was not one to stop at anything (see 1 Kings 21). Not surprisingly, Elijah was frightened by her threat (19:3).

He went a day's journey south into the wilderness, sat down, and asked that he might die (19:4; cf. Jonah 3:4; 4:3, 9). *"I am no better than my fathers,"* i.e., as good as dead (see 19:10, 14). This is quite a letdown after his tremendous victory, and it might be thought that God's astounding intervention at Mt. Carmel would have given Elijah confidence that God could now spare him from the machinations of Jezebel. But just as Israel, after the great deliverance by the sea, lapsed into complaining and mistrust, so here, Elijah gives way to anxiety and self-pity. It is not said that he was hungry—though after his phenomenal run to Jezreel (18:46) and day's journey into the wilderness, he might well have been. As with Israel in the wilderness, so here, God provides food for Elijah: not manna, but a "cake baked on hot stones and a jar of water," brought by an angel (cf. Bel and the Dragon 34–36). *"And he ate, and drank, and lay down again."* There is no reason to think that the food was supernatural. A later apocalyptic and messianic text possibly alludes to the situation of Elijah, but is transformed into hope for the resurrection of the dead and, perhaps, a messianic meal: "And with that Son of man shall they eat and lie down and rise up for ever and ever" (Enoch 62:14). After he rested, the angel again came, perhaps with more food and drink, and urged him to partake in preparation for the long journey ahead. "In the strength of that food," without eating anything else, it seems, Elijah then went forty days and forty nights, as later, Jesus did, in Matthew's story of his "temptation in the wilderness" (Matt. 4:1–2). Elijah's destination was Mt. Horeb, the mountain of God where Moses received the law, as it is named in E and Deuteronomic tradition (Exod. 3:1; Deut. 5:2). Here Moses also had spent forty days and forty nights (Exod. 24:18; 34:28). In this setting, later in the chapter, the "still small voice" of the Lord calls Elijah from his self-pity and dejection, to go forth and anoint Hazael to be king over Syria (!), Jehu to be king over Israel, and Elisha to be his own successor as prophet.

Second Lesson: Eph. 4:30–5:2. These verses are part of the section on Christian living or ethics that runs from 4:1 through 6:9 The pericope begins with "And" (4:30), while 5:3 begins with "But" *(de)*, indicating, as does content analysis, continuity with the preceding and following exhortations.

"Do not grieve the Holy Spirit" (4:30a): The Spirit is associated with the unity of the church (4:3–4). Evil talk (4:29) together with other forms of dissension (4:31) contrary to unity or community in the church would thus grieve the Holy Spirit. "In whom you were sealed for the day of redemption" (4:30b): This phrase recapitulates the declarations made in 1:13-14. Those who "believed in him [Christ] were sealed with the promised Holy Spirit." The understanding is that those who read the letter had received the "seal" of the Holy Spirit when (or shortly after) they first believed, possibly at the time of baptism (4:5). The Holy Spirit, moreover, is understood as "the guarantee of our inheritance until we acquire possession of it" (1:14). "Inheritance" *(klēronomia/nachalah)* is used in the OT for promised land, and in the NT for the "eternal inheritance," i.e., "salvation," e.g., Eph. 5:5. This is probably the sense of "the day of redemption" at 4:30b. These references (1:14; 4:30; and 5:5) are the principal suggestions in the letter as to future eschatological fulfillment. As in Gal. 5:21, so in Eph. 5:5 the author warns that those who practice immorality will not "inherit" the kingdom of God.

V. 31 picks up the thought of v. 26: Anger may be inevitable, but it is to be put away, along with kindred feelings and expressions of bitterness, wrath, clamor, slander, and malice. The readers are called to be "kind" or "gracious" *(chrēstoi)* to one another, goodhearted, and "freely giving" or "forgiving" *(charizomenoi)*, just as God in Christ "gave freely" (to) or "forgave" them (4:32). This *didachē* closely parallels Col. 3:12–13. It is also similar to Paul's admonitions to the Galatians in Gal. 5:16–23, where he calls on them to renounce the works of the flesh (including enmity, strife, jealousy, anger, dissension), and to manifest the fruit of the Spirit: "love, joy, peace, patience, kindness, goodness, faithfulness, gentleness, self-control." Paul does not generally speak of God's forgiveness, but rather of justification or reconciliation (e.g., Rom. 5:8–11). But the teaching of 4:31–32 is characteristic of the Pauline "indicative/imperative."

So is the exhortation to "walk in love, as Christ loved us and gave himself for us" (5:2). In Gal. 5:16, Paul called on his readers to "walk by the Spirit." The idiom, "to walk" is Hebraic, referring to the manner of conduct. As in Eph. 4:24, so in 5:1 f., he summons the readers to imitate God in mutual self-giving love (cf. Rom. 5:8; Phil. 2:1–8). The expression "beloved children," and the call to love as Christ loved us are reminiscent also of Johannine exhortation or paranesis: John 13:33–35; 1 John 4:9–11. The phrase "a fragrant offering and sacrifice to God" is used by Paul in Phil. 4:18, referring to the money the Philippian church has sent for the Jerusalem church. Paul does not describe Jesus' death in such terms elsewhere.

Gospel: John 6:41–51. In view of the earlier allusions in John 6 to Israel in the wilderness, it may be that the author referred to the "murmuring" of "the Jews" against Jesus (6:41) with the earlier "murmuring" of Israel (Exodus 16) in mind. John's Gospel dates from a period when Christians had drawn apart from Judaism; the author commonly sets "the Jews" over against Jesus, as if Jesus' own first followers—and he himself —had not also been Jews. (See, for example, 6:49: "*Your* fathers . . .") They protest that they know Jesus' parents: how then can he have "come down from heaven"? (John 6:42; see also 7:27). Reference here, and at Luke 4:22, to Jesus' father indicates that he may still have been alive at the time.

Instead of answering their rhetorical question, Jesus warns them not to murmur, and makes a series of statements about himself, God, and eternal life (6:43–51). Only those can come to Jesus who are drawn or led by God (v. 44). This is not strictly predestinarian, but God's grace or initiative is primary (see also 6:65). Such persons, Jesus says, "I will raise up at the last day." That Jesus himself, rather than God, will raise men from the dead at the resurrection is intimated only in this Gospel (see also 12:32). Some commentators, following Bultmann, propose that such references to "the last days" were not part of the original Gospel of John, where emphasis centers on the fact that the Son has already come, so that judgment, resurrection, and eternal life are already present possibilities. Others see the tension between actualized and futuristic eschatology as a basic feature of the original gospel. V. 45, picking up from v. 44a, also emphasizes the priority of God's initiative, but inclusively, rather than restrictively: "Everyone who has heard and learned from the Father comes to me." But no one has *seen* the Father, "except him who is from God" (v. 46), i.e., Jesus himself (cf. 1:1–5, 18).

Again (as in vv. 29, 35, 40), the stress is upon *believing in* Jesus: "He who believes has eternal life" (v. 47). The fathers ate bread in the wilderness, but they died (v. 49). Jesus as "the bread of life" (v. 48) or "living bread" (v. 51), gives eternal life. The conception of the eucharist as "medicine of immortality," formulated soon afterwards by Ignatius of Antioch, may be anticipated in these verses: "If anyone eats of this bread, he will live for ever" (v. 51; see also vv. 50, 54). Yet is should be noted that the Fourth Evangelist often writes in "figures" and attributes such also to Jesus (e.g., 10:6). In John 4:32–34, "food" represents Jesus' doing the will of God. In chap. 6, it may be that "eating bread," identified with Jesus, is a metaphor for believing in him, which itself, without sacramental partaking, leads to eternal life (6:40, 47). As the manna came down from heaven, so did Jesus (3:13; 6:38, 51).

HOMILETICAL INTERPRETATION

First Lesson: 1 Kings 19:4–8. It seems that an enraged and humiliated Jezebel is more terrifying to Elijah than forty-five prophets of Baal; be that as it may, Elijah is seized by despair, futility, weariness—and panic. He is both "beating a retreat" (fleeing) and "making a retreat" (going into solitude to seek renewal). While concerned to put distance between himself and the threatening queen, he does not, however, flee to strange lands like Jonah, but flees deliberately—and no doubt with subconscious promptings—to the place of Israel's origins. In that sacred place of "beginning" he will either die or be renewed.

Whenever some great task or crisis faces us, our immediate reaction is to say, "I am not able." Our energies retreat, draw back to the fountainhead, back to our subconscious. It is a symbolic return to the beginning . . . and that is at once the point of danger and the point of potential renewal. We can get stuck "back there" in the "beginning": the world of babyhood and infancy, the world of dependency and security, for it is a nostalgic and romantic world full of the earliest and therefore the most potent memories; or, going back, we can be reborn, rediscover ourselves, find again the adventurous motives of life and purpose.

This whole process is played out in Elijah's symbolic (note the "forty days and forty nights") return to Horeb, the place of Israel's beginnings. Utterly weary, the threat of Jezebel is the "last straw." Can one never do enough? Must one crisis follow on the heels of another? Why does it happen to me? Why does God allow a spectacular victory to be turned into humiliating defeat? It is too much: "O Lord, take away my life." Self-deprecation sets in: "I am no better than my fathers" (which perhaps is really an excuse, "Don't expect me to be better than . . ."), and that exactly marks the danger of this return: for if I am no better I may as well stay with my fathers and make no new ventures.

Yet one *must* go back all the way . . . and that nostalgic pull enables us to do so.

Unfortunately, the pericope ends back there "at the beginning." While we know that Elijah eventually rediscovered his sources, all we can do on the basis of this pericope is to show the possibility of his doing so.

Back there, where Israel began, he can also begin again. So we can go back to our own sources, to the fountainhead of our faith, our tradition —not to remain there, parroting old formulae, but to begin again with the tasks at hand in our time.

Second Lesson: Eph. 4:30–5:2. Elijah (First Lesson) makes his return to the place of beginnings; here, the writer calls the Ephesians to make a similar return to their beginnings. The process of change (transformation, see Pentecost 11, Eph. 4:17-24) necessitates again and again at least a look backwards in order to check or reestablish bearings. It is always from that "place of beginnings" that one works forward to deal with the tasks at hand.

It is in precisely this fashion that the writer frames and expresses his admonitions. He doesn't, in parental or authoritarian fashion, simply issue commands. He says, "Do not grieve the Holy Spirit *because* you are authentically certified to be God's heritage." To get the full effect, we need to turn that around: "*Because* you are . . . therefore do not grieve . . ."; "*Because* God in Christ forgave you, therefore be tender . . ."; "*Because* you are beloved children, therefore imitate God"; "*Because* Christ loved us, therefore walk in love." The "indicative" is the basis of the "imperative." Someone has called this the "grammar of the Gospel" in distinction to the "grammar of the Law" which proceeds conditionally: "If . . . then . . .," "If you want to be forgiven, then forgive others."

It is in this way that the writer recalls the Ephesians to their "place of beginnings": "You *are*, now become what you are." You are marked as God's possession; you are forgiven; you are beloved children; you are loved . . . now let that show!

Our world and our society constantly "put us down." Like Elijah we grow weary, and our self-image erodes. "You are only the son of Joseph, the carpenter, from Nazareth. How can you offer anything?" (Gospel, John 6:41-51). Small wonder we are ready to give up, and to give vent (v. 29) to "bitterness and wrath and anger and clamor and slander" (v. 31). Of course this reveals our impotence—like the raging child who is reduced to name-calling; but the sensitive ear will hear in all that clamor the plea for recognition. And hearing that plea, the fruitful response is that of affirmation: "You are . . . Remember your place of beginnings: return there and begin again."

Gospel: John 6:41–51. Wrestling with this passage can make "murmurers" of us, too! Who can make sense of it? But that should be a warning: by trying so hard to make sense of it we may block profounder understanding. It was not the "Flat Earth Society" members who discovered the new world, but those who dared to imagine new dimensions.

We are rather prone to be "Flat God Society" members for whom God is a one-dimensional book or code or metaphysical formula. The Incarnation is still as great an offense as ever it was. Oh, it's easy enough to say Jesus was God incarnate—but can we get beyond the one-dimensionality of such a statement? Can we perceive God in the last, the least, and the lost (cf. Matt. 25:31 ff.)? Can we truly acknowledge the human (a son of Joseph!) as the vehicle for the divine? Can we dare to hear a human word as divine Word when it confronts us with judgment and/or heals us with grace?

We listen but do not genuinely hear. We do not hear because we do not believe—do not trust God as the Father who teaches directly and not by codified transmissions. Those transmissions are there, true (like the "prophets"), but they suggest, provoke, stimulate, point beyond themselves to the always incarnated word. To stop with the letter of the transmissions is to expect the Messiah to leap off the pinnacle of the temple, is to want to store up manna for the next day. That way lies disillusionment, for "signs" only whet the appetite for more signs, and stored manna becomes wormy.

After Moses and the prophets, how is it that more witnesses are demanded? After the Incarnation, how many more witnesses to God's saving presence in the world do we need? Having heard these witnesses, how is it that we cannot hear God in the human voice of the world? The offense of Incarnation!

Manna is a good case in point. "The Jews" saw it only as a "sign," an interesting marvel Moses did (6:30 ff.); they failed to see God in, with, under, and beyond it. It never became "transfigured" for their one-dimensional eyes, never became a vehicle for the saving life of God which he was sharing with his people. It is like that with Jesus. While "the Jews" saw him only as son of Joseph, we see him equally statically as Son of God. Can they and we see the life of God manifested and shared through humanity? Jesus says, "I *am* the living bread because I *give* it." When we in our life-together give each other "bread," can we celebrate that as God's saving presence among us? That is the offense of Incarnation!

The Thirteenth Sunday after Pentecost

Lutheran	Roman Catholic	Episcopal	Pres./UCC/Chr.	Methodist/COCU
Prov. 9:1–6	Prov. 9:1–6	Prov. 9:1–6	Prov. 9:1–6	Prov. 9:1–6
Eph. 5:15–20	Eph. 5:15–20	Eph. 5:15–20	Eph. 5:15–20	Eph. 5:15–20
John 6:51–58	John 6:51–59	John 6:53–58	John 6:51–59	John 6:51–59

EXEGESIS

First Lesson: Prov. 9:1–6. Wisdom, thought of as a feminine person,
is described in Proverbs 8 as the first being created by God, who was
with him, helping design and construct the universe (8:22–31). Prov. 9:1
possibly refers to this role: Wisdom, the master workman or, more precisely, "like a master workman" (8:30), has "built her house" and "set up
her seven pillars." "House" may refer to the world, the pillars to those
columns on which the sky is suspended (see Job 26:11). Or, it may refer,
metaphorically, to her royal palace on earth, whence she speaks to those
who will hear, and to which she calls those who will come.

"*She has slaughtered her beasts . . .*" (vv. 2–6): Wisdom has prepared
a banquet, and sent her maidservants to summon all in town to eat of her
bread, and drink her wine. We have here an allegory or parable rather
like the Parable of the Great Supper (Luke 14:15–24) to which all are
invited. There, the house and the banquet represent salvation in the
kingdom of God. But not everyone will "eat bread in the kingdom of
God" (Luke 14:15); only those who respond to the invitation, or when
they fail to do so, those who are compelled to come in. In Proverbs, it
is also a question of salvation, but thought of in a different way.

V. 4 exactly duplicates v. 16, later in the chapter. The latter is the
invitation of the foolish, shameless, wanton woman (a harlot), who calls
"from the highest places of the town" (9:14–15; cf. 9:3), trying to seduce
male passersby to their unwitting destruction. In contrast, Wisdom invites
those who are "simple" and "without sense" to eat of her bread, and
drink of her wine (cf. v. 17), which means, to "leave simpleness," "walk
in the way of insight" which leads to life (v. 6). This parable illustrates
the basic understanding of the wisdom theology, which is that the
righteous (those who heed wisdom) shall have their reward in prosperity
and long life, while the foolish, who give way to wickedness, shall suffer
adversity and an early death. (Thus, e.g., Prov. 12:7, 21; 14:11; Psalm
37). As in the Book of Deuteronomy and the earlier prophets, so in the
wisdom writings, the individual is summoned to insight, wisdom, knowledge, and righteousness, all of which have their beginning in "the fear
of the Lord" (9:10).

Second Lesson: Eph. 5:15–20. We have more here from the extended section of exhortations on Christian living in Eph. 4:1–6:9. As in 5:2 and 5:8, the term "to walk" refers to conduct. The contrast between "wise" and "foolish" resembles the terminology of the wisdom writings (esp. Proverbs and Ecclesiasticus where wise = righteous, and foolish = wicked.

"Making the most of the time": This expression may derive from Col. 4:5. It probably refers to the expectation which is not, however, particularly emphasized in Ephesians, that the end of this age and the beginning of the age to come is near (cf. 1:13–14, 21b). *"Because the days are evil"* (v. 16b): As in the synoptic Gospels and 1 John, Satan's power, if not dominion, on earth is taken seriously. The "prince of the power of the air," an evil spirit, probably *the* evil spirit, the devil (6:11), "is now at work in the sons of disobedience" (Eph. 2:2). The devil and his "principalities and powers" are the rulers of the world in its present darkness (6:12; cf. 1 John 5:19 and Gal. 1:4). But the evil one and his horde can be resisted by "putting on the whole armor of God": truth, righteousness, the gospel of peace, "above all" the "shield of faith," salvation, and the spirit (6:10–17). Because time is short, and the days evil, it is all the more important not to be foolish, but to "understand what the will of the Lord is" (5:17). The will of "the Lord" may refer to God or Christ; textual variants support both readings. In any event, it is probably understood to refer to the whole range of matters reviewed in chaps. 4–6, if not the letter as a whole and Paul's other writings and the Gospels.

The readers are cautioned to renounce the way of false joy or enthusiasm: getting drunk with wine, for that is "debauchery" (RSV) or, more precisely, "wastefulness" *(asōtia).* Paul elsewhere had cautioned that those who engage in "drunkenness" and "carousing" would not inherit the kingdom of God (Gal. 5:21). Instead (of being filled with wine), Christians are to be filled with the Spirit. Their joy and celebration are to be experienced and expressed in psalms, hymns, and spiritual songs (Eph. 5:19). Thus they are to address one another, we infer, in coherent and edifying expressions of the Spirit (cf. 1 Cor. 14). And they are to address, or sing to and praise the Lord joyfully, "in [or "with"] their heart."

Vv. 19 and 20 closely parallel Col. 3:16–17, as do the admonitions to wives, husbands, children, slaves, and masters that follow in each letter (Eph. 5:21–6:9; Col. 3:18–4:1), indicating probable literary dependence. The instruction to give thanks "always" and "for everything" is certainly characteristic of Paul, who based it on his assurance that death, sin, and the law have been overcome by Christ (1 Cor. 15:51–58), and that the coming of the Lord is near (Phil. 4:4–6).

Gospel: John 6:51–59. The first two-thirds of v. 51 accords with the apparently metaphorical description of Jesus as the bread of life which came down from heaven, to which one may come and eat (= believe), and so have eternal life (e.g., John 6:35-40, 47-50). But in vv. 51c-57, a more literally sacramental or eucharistic meaning seems to be asserted (see esp. v. 55). Six references to Jesus' "flesh" *(sarx)* are featured here, four associated with the verb "to eat," the other two with "food" or "bread." With these references to Jesus' (or the Son of man's) flesh are four suggestions or invitations to drink his blood. Those who eat Jesus' flesh and drink his blood (cf. v. 57, "he who eats me") have eternal life. All this would seem to refer to the eucharistic eating and drinking of bread and wine, understood as Jesus' body and blood, after the fashion of Ignatius' conception of the eucharist as the "medicine of immortality," if not also the idea of transubstantiation. Consequently, on critical if not also dogmatic grounds, Bultmann considers the passage a secondary interpolation intended to add emphasis to the eucharist which is otherwise lacking in the Gospel.

Elsewhere in John, the basic understanding is that *believing in* Jesus (or Christ) is the way to eternal life (e.g., 3:16, 17; 6:29, 35, 40, 47). In John 6:40, Jesus states that it is God's will that everyone who believes in him "should have eternal life, and I will raise him up at the last day"; but at 6:54, that *"he who eats my flesh and drinks my blood* has eternal life, and I will raise him up at the last day." The prospect of eternal life and resurrection is constant in both cases, but the "means of grace" seem different. The expression, "abides in me, and I in him" (v. 56) is characteristically Johannine; but in other contexts it is not used in a eucharistic sense, but rather in reference to Jesus' and God's love and commandments (John 15:4-10; 1 John 2:6; 3:24; 4:12-16). It is a question, then, whether the language about eating Jesus' flesh and drinking his blood was intended literally, i.e., sacramentally, or as a still more concrete or vivid version of the metaphor: eating the bread of life, which is Jesus = "seeing" or "coming to" him and believing in him. It does seem that v. 58 picks up again the more symbolic understanding expressed in 6:27-51b. Jesus, like the "bread" or manna in the wilderness, "came down from heaven"; the fathers ate that bread but died; but "he who eats *this* bread (= believes in Jesus) will live forever" (cf. esp. v. 51a-b).

HOMILETICAL INTERPRETATION

First Lesson: Prov. 9:1-6. We have here an appeal to partake of Wisdom's feast, i.e., to benefit from the experience of man's past and our own past, rather than continue being stupid and acting stupidly (contrast Folly's feast, 9:13-18). Heaven knows, we need to be wise today; our greedy exploitation of the earth and its natural resources, our insane economic policies of constant growth and constant consumption, our inhuman abuse of peoples are all very stupid—and deep down we know it. We sup at Folly's table, while Wisdom's feast goes unattended; we are fools, not wise persons (cf. Second Lesson).

Thankfully, we are beginning to realize the urgent need to be wise; and yet it is there we touch the heart of an ancient dilemma: knowing does not guarantee doing. Perhaps that is why Israel's wise men eventually connected wisdom with God himself, even personifying it to stress this connection, and thereby making the point that wisdom is attainable *only* from God.

We are, I think, again at that stage. Our technology raises the serious question whether our vaunted wisdom is really wise. For if it were, it wouldn't constantly backfire on us. The results of our "wisdom" leave us with ever new and more devastating threats to life; our well-intentioned efforts produce monstrous Frankensteins. To begin now to ponder afresh what it means that wisdom is a gift from God will be a hard process. It may demand a confession of our bankruptcy, and thus an uncomfortable humility and tentativeness about our "way of life" and our personal and corporate "rights." It will require a renewed struggle with the problem of how to live and work in the world while yet acknowledging the overarching priorities of God (cf. Paul's discussion of "wisdom" and "foolishness" in 1 Cor. 1:18-25); of how to keep our feet on the ground while yet trusting in his guidance of the world (cf. Jesus' admonition to be "wise as serpents and innocent as doves," Matt. 10:16).

Central to this struggle will be our conception of God. This text assumes that God blesses the wise person's righteousness, and punishes the fool's wickedness. Popular theology—even as it is played out in national and international councils—assumes the same (e.g., "the poor are poor because they are lazy, stupid, etc."). In the end that makes God an enemy of man. But the God of Jesus Christ is *not* our enemy, he is not a competitor. God, to use a strange phrase, has built himself into our human life, he has not just added himself on to it. That is what the personified Wisdom of the text is getting at, and that is what the Incarnation demonstrates and expresses.

Second Lesson: Eph. 5:15-20. This lesson, like the First Lesson, urges us to be wise, and goes on to show us how the gift of wisdom is received from God: cast out your foolishness, it says, and "be filled with the Spirit."

The foolish person does not know what time it is, nor who he is, and thus does not know what to do (what the will of the Lord is). A consistent mark of the authentic prophet was his ability to discern the time: the right time to speak, the opportune moment to act. He knew, in short, when the *kairos* arrived. Foolishness manifests itself most vividly in its misjudgment of or insensitivity to the right time. Even a right word at a wrong time misses its mark. "The days are evil," true; the wise person knows when the opportunity arrives to counteract that evil. The foolish person, secondly, does not know who he is, and thus is not only "out of character" but worse, characterless. The wise person knows he is "sealed," forgiven, a beloved child (Pentecost 12, Eph. 4:30–5:2), "light in the Lord" (5:8). Finally, the foolish person does not know "what the will of the Lord is." Of course not, because the will of the Lord emerges out of the matrix wherein we, knowing who we are, engage the *kairos*. This engagement will certainly demand risk; at the same time it will reveal any pretensions and arrogance we have—but that is part of discovering what is the will of the Lord.

"Empty out this foolishness and be filled with the Spirit." That sounds charismatic, ecstatic, even glossollalic; these dimensions surely may be involved. It certainly sounds "pious" in the negative sense the word has acquired: Who wants to go around singing hymns? While it might be interesting to try, few of us are prepared to do so. At any rate, the emptying out of foolishness and the filling up of the Spirit are of one piece with Eph. 4:17–24 (Pentecost 11) and 4:30–5:2 (Pentecost 12): a change from one lifestyle to another, and that at very practical levels. What comes out of a man, Jesus remarked, is what is already in him, and language is surely an immediate indicator of the content of the heart. Thus the language of the Spirit-filled person, of the new lifestyle, will be characterized by joy and celebration, a language that cherishes, respects, reverences, affirms, heals. Secondly, this new language will demonstrate a new attitude, that of thankfulness. An aged Amerindian woman said, "Wherever the white man touches the world, he leaves it sore." Would thankfulness halt our trails of environmental and human soreness?

Gospel: John 6:51–58. There are many ways in which we humans can and do explain the meaning and purpose of our existence and express our hopes for some kind of salvation. For example, we can take a naturalistic stance and tell a story of a seed germinating, flowering, bearing fruit, and dying, and say that that is the story of human existence. Or, we can take the stance of faith and tell a story of "God and his relationships with man." The Scriptures clearly tell such a "faith story," and, for the Fourth Gospel, as for all the NT writers, this story is essentially embodied in Jesus of Nazareth. The realistic (cannibalistic!) language of the evangelist preserves the insistent claim of the church that the historical Jesus is the mediator of God's eternal life, accomplished through his death on the cross. A specific life was given, in history, for the life of the world. At the same time, the life that was given transcends history, or, better, incorporates history: quite specifically that means that the meaning and purpose of my life and my hopes for redemption and salvation are to be found in the story of Jesus of Nazareth.

That is, of course, an affront to me. After all, I come from a good family (Abraham . . . Peter . . . Luther . . . Calvin!); I have a proud history (Red Sea . . . baptism!); I have had profound experiences (Manna . . . the "bread" of the Torah . . . the eucharist!). I have life, I know the ultimate meaning of life, I know what the will of the Lord is. My own life is measure enough; it is sufficient standard and norm. All I want is a little "extra" to corroborate my story: a "sign" or two to show me I'm on the right track; a baptismal certificate to hang on the wall; a fragment of bread and a sip of wine . . .

The evangelist says, "No! Unless you eat the flesh of the Son of man and drink his blood you have no life in you." My story, no matter how noble, is not sufficient to incorporate the height and depth and length and breadth of life under God, nor is it sufficient to offer redemption to the world. Even the story of a people (Israel, church) is not sufficient. So the evangelist points us beyond these stories to the greater story of Jesus in whom all our lesser stories find fulfillment and correction. Our eucharists and baptisms and Bibles push us into that larger story. His images flow one into the other: flesh and blood are the same as door, vine, bread, water, light—all of which represent Jesus in his ultimate significance. To eat and drink are the same as "abiding in," "coming to," "believing in," "having life," "seeing," that is, full participation in the story of Jesus, realizing it (i.e., making it real) in our lives, realizing it (i.e., discovering its reality) in our own existence.

The Fourteenth Sunday after Pentecost

8/22

Lutheran	Roman Catholic	Episcopal	Pres./UCC/Chr.	Methodist/COCU
Josh. 24:1-2a,	Josh. 24:1-2a,	Josh. 24:1-2a,	Josh. 24:14-18	Josh. 24:1-2a,
14-18	15-17, 18b	14-18		14-18
Eph. 5:21-31	Eph. 5:21-32	Eph. 5:21-32	Eph. 5:21-33	Eph. 5:21-33
John 6:60-69	John 6:61-70	John 6:60-69	John 6:60-69	John 6:60-69

EXEGESIS

First Lesson: Josh. 24:1-2, 14-18. As the story is told in the Book of Joshua, the Israelites defeated the indigenous population of the land of Canaan (chaps. 1-12), after which Joshua allotted each tribe its own territory (chaps. 13-22). Chaps. 23-24 report Joshua's "farewell address" to the tribes of Israel considerably later (23:1), and shortly before his death (24:29). Chap. 23 is generally attributed to the Deuteronomistic Historian (RD or DH); chap. 24 to the old Northern or Elohist (E) tradition.

Historians have found evidence suggesting an annual ceremony of covenant renewal in ancient Israel during the days of the Judges (ca. 1200-1000 BC), when the leaders or elders of the tribes would gather, if possible at Shechem, to hear the reading of the Covenant (Law), and exhortations to keep it faithfully (Deuteronomy 6-11), after which, seated on Mts. Ebal and Gerizim, they would shout blessings and curses upon themselves—the latter as sanction lest they fail to keep the ordinances and statutes (see Deut. 11:26–29; chaps. 27–30; Josh. 8:30–35). Part of this ceremony, Gerhard von Rad has proposed, consisted of a recitation of the "cultic credo," reviewing the great acts of God on behalf of his people in the past in fulfillment of his promises to the patriarchs. This "credo" or recitation of God's acts has been preserved in three versions, according to von Rad: at Deut. 26:5–9, Deut. 6:20–23, and a more detailed or expanded statement, at Josh. 24:2–13.

Whether read as the last words of Joshua to the tribes of Israel on this particular occasion, or as a confession of faith deriving from the ancient renewal ceremony at Shechem (mentioned in Josh. 24:1, 25), the statement in vv. 2–13 testifies to Israel's belief that it was the Lord (Yahweh) who called them into being and sustained them, beginning beyond "the flood" (Euphrates) with Abraham (24:2), through Egypt and exodus, wilderness and enemy peoples, into possession of the land.

Following the conclusion of the "credo" (v. 13,), Joshua exhorts the people assembled to fear the Lord, serve him and him alone, sincerely and faithfully. "Choose this day whom you will serve" (v. 15): Here is a great summons to faithfulness and obedience to God, epitomizing the central theme of the prophetic (e.g., Elijah, Hosea) and Deuteronomistic paranesis. "But as for me and my house, we will serve the Lord." Joshua (or the leader of the congregation) declares his own choice: devotion to the Lord. The people respond—possibly in the words of the renewal ceremony's liturgy—with a shortened form of the "cultic credo" (vv. 17–18a), and their own pledge, renouncing service to other gods, and dedicating themselves to serve Yahweh, "for he is our God" (vv. 16, 18b).

Second Lesson: Eph. 5:21–33. The basic concerns of the author of Ephesians are the unity of the church, and the faithful moral life of its members. The author now turns to the subject of the right attitude and conduct of husbands and wives toward one another (cf. Col. 3:18–19), and compares this with the relation between Christ and church.

"Be subject to one another in (reverent) fear *(phobos)* of Christ" (v. 21): The principle here is mutual submissiveness, in recognition of the lordship of Christ over all. But then the writer calls on wives to be subject to their husbands, "just as" *(hōs)* to Christ (vv. 22–24). There is no doubt that Paul regarded wives as second in authority to husbands: woman was made from man and *for* man (1 Cor. 11:8–9). However, the analogy, husband is head of wife as Christ is head of church, is not found in the incontrovertibly Pauline letters. Instead, we find the principle—if not consistently applied—of full equality in Christ: Gal. 3:28; cf. Col. 3:11.

But it is not only a matter of *subjection.* Husbands are to *love* their wives as Christ loved the church (v. 25). The theological affirmations about Christ's self-giving love for and cleansing of the church (vv. 25b–27) are unusual. In Paul's letters, reference usually is to Christ's (or God's) love or self-giving "for us" (Rom. 5:8; 1 Cor. 15:3, 57; Gal. 3:13; 4:3–5), for "the world" (2 Cor. 5:19; cf. John 3:16), for "many" (Rom. 5:15), or for "all" (Rom. 5:18; 11:32; 2 Cor. 5:14–15), but not "for the church." "Having cleansed her by the washing of water with the word . . ." (v. 26): Perhaps "water" here represents baptism, though elsewhere Paul speaks of baptism in association with the "one Spirit" (1 Cor. 12:13) or "into Christ" (Gal. 3:27). Here the association is with "the word" *(hrēma),* which may suggest that the cleansing of the church is through Christ's and, perhaps, the apostles' instruction or teaching. The conception of the church as the bride of Christ also appears in 2 Cor. 11:2, though as a simile, and with reference to the Corinthian church in particular; cf. the eschatological holy city, Jerusalem, "coming down . . . prepared *as* a bride adorned for her husband" (Rev. 21:2).

V. 28 returns to husbands and wives, with the argument that since man and woman are "one flesh" (Gen. 2:24), "he who loves his wife loves himself." Moreover, both are members of Christ's body (v. 29). Vv. 29b–32 again take up the love of Christ for his church, interpreting Gen. 2:24 allegorically, "to mean Christ and the church." But "even if" *(plēn)* this is its intended meaning, the writer says, each one should love his wife "as himself"; (cf. Lev. 19:18), and the wife should "respect" *(phōbetai:* reverently "fear") the husband.

Gospel: John 6:60–70.
Perhaps some of the disciples had been absent during Jesus' discourse with "the Jews" about the bread of life (6:25–59), and only later (v. 60) heard about it. Many of them now complain, "This is a hard saying" (v. 60). It is not clear whether "this" refers to the saying at 6:57, the whole series of sayings in 6:51c–57, or the more symbolic saying at v. 58. Jesus' reply corresponds more to the symbolic or allegorical sayings in 6:27–51b, 58, than to the apparently eucharist sayings in vv. 51c–57. If the disciples "take offense" (lit., "are scandalized") at "this," how would they react to his (the Son of man's) *"ascending* where he was before" (vv. 61–62)? "This," in vv. 60 and 61 would seem, then, to refer to Jesus' claim that he *came down* from heaven (6:33, 38, 50, 51a, 58a), the claim that had also occasioned the "murmuring" of "the Jews" (6:41–42).

V. 63 apparently repudiates the kind of materialistic and eucharistic understanding represented in 6:51c–57. The *"flesh* is of no avail," it is "the spirit that gives life." The *words* Jesus has *spoken* to them "are spirit and life" (cf. v. 68). On the basis of these words, the disciples should have believed, "but there are some of you who do not believe" (v. 64). Here, as in numerous other verses in 6:27–51, the way of life is to believe in Jesus; in that sense he is "bread of life" to those who "eat," i.e., believe in him. (So also John 3:16.) It is almost as if vv. 63–64 had

been written to counter or correct the apparent literalism and sacra-
mentalism of John 6:51c–57, where *believing* is not mentioned. V. 65
continues the thought of v. 64a: here as elsewhere in chap. 6, "coming
to" Jesus is equivalent to "believing in" him (cf. vv. 44a, 47). As generally
in this Gospel, Jesus knows in advance what is to happen: here, who will
not believe, and who will betray him (vv. 64b, 70–71). .
    "*After this many of his disciples drew back . . .*" (v. 66): The more
"spiritual" interpretation of vv. 51-57 given in vv. 61-65 evidently does
not satisfy them. These disciples, not specifically identified with "the
Jews" (v. 52), represent a larger circle of followers than the twelve. After
"many" of them left, Jesus asks the twelve if they, too, will go away.
Peter responds for them with a confession of faith which some interpreters regard as John's equivalent to Peter's "confession" at Caesarea
Philippi (Mark 8:27-30): "You have the words of eternal life; and we
have believed, and come to know, that you are the Holy One of God"
(vv. 68–69). Jesus' words are the basis for belief. They, not eucharistic
food, give eternal life. Not only have the disciples *believed,* they have
come to *know* who Jesus is (cf. 1:10b).

HOMILETICAL INTERPRETATION

First Lesson: Josh. 24:1–2a, 14–18. It is highly significant that when
the chronicler proceeds to record the "last will and testament" of Joshua,
he has Joshua tell a story (24:1-13). It is the familiar story which begins
with Abraham and moves on through the captivity in Egypt to the
exodus and the conquest of Canaan.
    Every community of people articulates its own history, and this his-
tory is essentially a story which is first told orally and eventually is recorded in writing. Such a story is always a profound interpretation of
human existence: by depicting a people's origins and the crucial events
which they have experienced it answers the basic religious questions of
"Who am I? Who are we? Why are we?" That is, their story affords a
people a common rootage, a common self-understanding, and a common
destiny. This story shapes a people, it gives them identity, makes them
distinctive, sets them apart; and it serves as a standard by which to understand and interpret subsequent events, and by which to assess other
stories, other interpretations of existence. It is ultimately a statement of
faith, which both preserves faith and creates faith.
    Such a story is never static—though always in danger of becoming
static, frozen in formula, closed. Periodically momentous events neces-
sitate a reinterpretation of the story. In the Judaic-Christian story, the
Babylonian Captivity, Jesus of Nazareth, the Reformation were such
times, and certainly our present chaotic era is again such a time.
    We, like Joshua's Israel assembled in their newly acquired land, are
poised in a "threshold" situation. We know where we have come from,
but we have only hints of what the world we have entered will be like.

It is then that we have doubts about the validity, the truthfulness, the relevance of our story, of our interpretation of human existence. Is our story adequate in this new world? Is the story of Yahweh covenanting with his people adequate to an agrarian Canaan? Is the story of Jesus and the church (note how the Gospels and the creed essentially tell a story!) adequate to a technological and pluralistic world? Can this story still shape us and hold us together? Can it still make meaning of our new existence? Above all, can it still save us and others from meaninglessness and fear and guilt?

Joshua believed Israel's story could, though he feared that his people might fall easy prey to the stories of Canaan. Jesus put the question to his followers (Gospel Lesson), and Peter's answer is affirmed to the Ephesian readers (Second Lesson).

Joshua's question is ever again our question: How will we tell our story? How we will interpret our existence? Which God will we choose to serve?

Second Lesson: Eph. 5:21–31. Suppose you are living in a society in which (1) marriage is held in light esteem and as a consequence degradation and de-humanization are corrosive forces; and (2) women are not even "second-class citizens." What analogy or model would you advance in order to expose and hopefully correct the situation?

It is not difficult to "suppose" such a society—it is very much our own. Nor is it difficult to select any number of explanations or rationalizations of marriage from the many being recommended and practiced today. A biological model suggests that marriage is only for the purpose of bearing children; prior to and apart from that task and after its completion marriage is unnecessary. A psychological model suggests that marriage is a mutually supportive structure, valid only so long as it indeed mutually supports. A sociological model suggests that marriage and the family are the bedrock units of a society. Further models grow out of romantic, sacramental, economic, and sometimes very exotic, soils. Are any of these, or even combinations of these, capable of doing the twofold task of exposing and correcting a bad marital situation in society?

The writer to the Ephesians laid hold of an extraordinary and singularly impressive model: the relationship between Christ and his body, the church. While we are hypersensitive to his seeming male chauvinism, we ought not allow this to blind us to the revolutionary power of his model. While he speaks of the husband as head of the wife even as Christ is head of the church, he takes pains to show that this does not mean *control*. He goes out of his way to stress that Christ saves, cleanses, sanctifies, nourishes, cherishes, and glorifies the church. If this is "power over" or "control over" it is indeed a very peculiar power and control!

If we can then discard the idea of control-obedience, we still find offensive that the husband should do this *for* the wife as Christ does it for

the church. We must admit that at this point the analogy breaks down.
The Pauline writer is conscious of the limitations of his analogy: at the
end he admits, "This is a great mystery!" Nevertheless, his point is powerful: marriage is a new and profound relationship, analogous to Christ
and the church. When the Spirit enters (cf. Pentecost 13, Eph. 5:15-20),
marriage too is transformed.

As an important event in life, marriage also poses the question, "How
will we interpret and tell our story?" (First Lesson). Shall it fall outside
our story (be simply biological or psychological, etc.), or become an
integral part of it? If part of it, then it must be incorporated into the
paradigmatic story, that of Christ and the church.

Gospel: John 6:60–69. The evangelist reviews the scope of his dialogue in swift fashion before posing the ultimate question. Again the
murmuring—but now there is a note of hard-nosed intolerance in it.
Jesus cuts through the murmuring and the earlier one-dimensionality:
"When I die and ascend, there will be no flesh and blood to see, much
less to eat and to drink. Then there will be only my spirit left, and my
words. *These* give life."

Joshua pleaded with his people (First Lesson) to remain faithful to
the "Yahwistic" story, to the traditional interpretation of the origin and
meaning of their existence. To depart from that story would mean de-
parting from their understanding of themselves as Yahweh's people, and
would result in disintegration. The evangelist has, in this chapter, set
forth a reinterpretation and a fulfillment of that same story: the story of
Israel is played out afresh, and to its fullest dimensions, in Jesus of
Nazareth: Passover (6:1-14, 51); Exodus crossing of Red Sea (6:16-21);
Covenant (6:56); wilderness wandering (6:25 ff.); Moses (6:14, 31-32,
49); the Promised Land (eternal life). It is still the *same story*, only now
the full dimensions of God's presence in it and his purposes are revealed.
If we murmur at eating his flesh and drinking his blood, this is the coun-
terpart to the murmurings done at the original Passover, exodus, wilderness wanderings, for it is a murmuring against a God who is too near.
We don't want a God who is too near: It seems unworthy of God to be
so closely identified with our world and our existence; furthermore, a God
so intensely near is threatening! Yet he *is* near. Even when Jesus is removed he will still be near. For Jesus, like manna in the desert or the
eucharist on the altar or the speaking of the prophets, has demonstrated
how near and involved God is. The removal of Jesus' physical presence,
the close of the eucharistic service, the end of the sermon, or the close of
a deeply communicative conversation, do not mean the close of an inti-
mate involvement with God. The event of Jesus Christ has shown once
and for all that God won't go away—he is present in all the interchanges
and interactions of life.

Faith is therefore required—not only in those special moments (like sacraments and sermon) but in all moments. Is the Joshua-Jesus story our story, or is it not? Is our personal story illumined, explained, directed, and transformed by that story, or is it not? In short, will we be God's people or some other kind of people? What is our credo, our story? The question is asked in an always dramatic setting: On the one hand the growing disaffection of Judas (apostasy in the First Lesson); on the other the tragedy of defection. The former plumbs the depths of evil consequences; the latter reveals the terrible blindness of not recognizing the true "sign" of God's presence to save.

The Fifteenth Sunday after Pentecost

Lutheran	*Roman Catholic*	*Episcopal*	*Pres./UCC/Chr.*	*Methodist/COCU*
Deut. 4:1–2, 6–8	Deut. 4:1–2, 6–8	Deut. 4:1–2, 6b–8	Deut. 4:1–8	Deut. 4:1–8
James 1:17–22 (23–25), 26–27	James 1:17–18, 21b–22, 27	James 1:17–18, 21b–22, 27	James 1:19–25	James 1:17–22, 26–27
Mark 7:1–8, 14–15, 21–23	Mark 7:1–8a, 14–15, 21–23	Mark 7:1–8, 14–15, 21–23	Mark 7:1–8, 14–15, 21–23	Mark 7:1–8, 14–15, 21–23

EXEGESIS

First Lesson: Deut. 4:1–2, (3–5), 6–8. The first four chapters of Deuteronomy consist of relatively late material, and probably were composed as a preface or introduction not only to the Decalogue (5:6–21) and the other laws in Deuteronomy, but to the entire "Deuteronomic History Book": Deuteronomy, Joshua, Judges, 1 and 2 Samuel, and 1 and 2 Kings. These writings were collected, revised, and arranged by an editor or editors influenced by the religious viewpoint of the Deuteronomic code (chaps. 12–26) and reform (ca. 622 BC), perhaps during the exile. These first four chapters present a narrative, as told by Moses to all Israel (Deut. 1:1, 5), reviewing what happened after the law was given at Mt. Horeb, as Israel moved on in the wilderness and into the land east of the Jordan River toward Jericho, and calling on Israel to obey this law.

It is not stated at 4:1, 2, 5, 6 or 8 *what* statutes, ordinances and commandments Israel is to keep, but as the book now stands, we can assume that the laws in question are those that follow in chap. 5, and particularly, chaps. 12–26, where the terms "commandments, ordinances, and statutes" are used in the preliminary and concluding exhortations (12:1; 26:16–19). A second collection of introductory exhortations or sermons follows in chaps. 6–11. Possibly some of these "sermons" date back to the ancient assemblies at Shechem in the days of the Judges (see above, Pentecost 14, First Lesson).

"That you may live, and go in and take possession of the land . . ." (4:1b): This is typical of the prophetic theology of history and also of the paranesis of Deuteronomy 6–11: the people can lose God's blessing if they fail to keep the covenant or laws which he has given them, particularly if they worship other gods. The laws are not to be added to or diminished (4:2a). Later rabbis understood that the law of Moses included 613 commandments. Jesus warned that the law was to remain in full force, without relaxation of even the least commandment (Matt. 5:18–19; cf. Luke 16:17). See also Rev. 22:18–19. The law is to be preserved as given so that the people will keep it as commanded (4:2, 5, 6a), and that it may go well with them in the land (4:40).

The incident at Baal-Peor is invoked as further sanction for keeping the covenant: God had destroyed those who worshiped Baal (Canaanite fertility god) there (Num. 25:1–9). The implication is that God will destroy those who worship other gods; cf. also, e.g., Deut. 4:26; 6:14–15; 7:3–4. Moreover, by keeping "all these statutes," Israel will commend itself in the eyes of other peoples, who will be impressed with their wisdom and understanding and the greatness of their nation which has such righteous statutes and ordinances (vv. 6–8).

Second Lesson: James 1:17–27. James is one of the "catholic" or general letters, addressed to all the churches, described metaphorically as "the twelve tribes of the dispersion" (1:1). The author does not claim to be James, the brother of Jesus, or even an apostle, but simply "a servant of God and of the Lord Jesus Christ" (1:1). He writes to encourage Christians to live in accordance with the "royal law" of love (2:8), patiently and helpfully in relation to others in the days of one's life (4:13–17), and in the time that remains until the coming of the Lord, which is near (5:7–9). God's grace is emphasized in 1:17–18. Every good and perfect gift is from God. The new life or creation which Christians enjoy is given by God who "of his own will . . . brought us forth by the word of truth."

"Let every man be quick to hear, slow to speak, slow to anger"(1:19b): In form, this balanced, triadic admonition is reminiscent of some of Jesus' sayings. James has more to say about speaking in 1:26 and 3:3–12. Here, he cautions particularly against anger: it does not "work the righteousness of God" (v. 20, cf. Gal. 5:20). All kinds of filthiness and evil (or "trouble," *kakia*), which may have been meant in relation either to speaking (cf. Mark 7:15–23; or to anger (cf. Matt. 5:22; Eph. 4:26, 31), are to be "put off" (cf. Eph. 4:22, 25).

"And receive with meekness the implanted word . . ." (1:21b): "Meekness" is in contrast to anger. The "implanted word" is the "word of truth" (v. 18), but whether this refers to Christ (John 1:14), the gospel

(Rom. 1:16), or Jesus' teaching (cf. Mark 4:14) is not certain. It is, in any case, the word that enables salvation. V. 22 suggests that it means the will of God: "Be doers of the word, and not hearers only" (cf. Matt. 7:21-27 = Luke 6:46-49; cf. Rom. 2:13). This is further suggested by the terms "perfect law," "law of liberty," and "royal law," which are equivalent, it seems, to the scriptural statement of the will of God, "You shall love your neighbor as yourself" (1:25, 2:8). Those who hear the word but do not do it, accomplish nothing and forget the word (vv. 23-25). The doer of the word does not forget, but acts; and "he shall be blessed in his doing" (cf. Matt. 5:3-10; 25:1-40).

Religion is not a matter of the tongue (1:26), whether thought of as mere talk, "filth" or gossip. Pure religion "before God" (v. 27) means both responsive action for one's neighbor—"to visit orphans and widows in their affliction"—and withdrawal from the contaminating influence of "the world" *(kosmos;* cf. 1 John 2:15-17).

Gospel: Mark 7:1–8, 14–15, 21–23. For about a hundred years, most scholars have regarded Mark as the earliest Gospel, dating its composition between A.D. 60 and 70. One of the great issues in NT criticism for nearly that long has been the question whether Mark's Gospel presents authentic reports of Jesus' words and actions, and to what extent it reflects the viewpoint of the church where it was composed and/or peculiar interests of its author-editor.

The controversy in 7:1-13 concerns the validity of the "tradition" or oral law of the Pharisees. Wishing to keep the written law, pious Jews as early, perhaps, as the first century B.C., had begun asking scribes to interpret its implications for certain situations not expressly defined therein. A body of such interpretations came to be passed on by word of mouth, initially, perhaps, to avoid confusion with the written law. This became known as "the tradition" or oral law, first written down, after A.D. 200, eventuating in the two Talmuds. In our Gospel Lesson, the scribes and Pharisees (traditionalists) ask Jesus why he does not require his disciples to wash their hands in accordance with the "tradition of the elders." Jesus' reply, quoting from Isa. 29:13 (LXX), distinguishes between the precepts or tradition *of men,* and the commandment of God. To illustrate, Jesus goes on, in vv. 9-13, to show that observance of "religious" practices may not be used as an excuse for refusing to assist one's parents in their need. Jesus elsewhere berates scribes and Pharisees for tending to minor, but neglecting the major parts of the law, for "straining out a gnat but swallowing a camel" (Matt. 23:23-24).

Jesus' attitude toward the law, and probably the oral tradition, is also suggested in the "antitheses" of Matt. 5:21-48. In these places, Jesus does not say that the law no longer applies; quite the opposite; Matt. 5:17-20; Luke 16:17; Matt. 23:23 = Luke 11:42. In Matthew, he even endorses the oral law of the scribes, though not their practice (23:3). But in Mark

7:1–8, if Jesus does not oppose the tradition regarding hand-washing, he certainly does not require his disciples to follow it.

In vv. 14–23, it is no longer a question about keeping the tradition. Rather, Jesus tells "the people" a "parable" (v. 17), namely, the saying given at v. 15. As with many of the parables in Mark, the disciples fail to understand, so Jesus has to explain the meaning to them: vv. 17–19, cf. 4:10–20, 33–34. Critics usually hold that these explanations are mainly Mark's own. This is clearly the case in 7:19b. The "parable" or riddle contrasts two kinds of defilement: ritual (from contact with "unclean" things), and that which arises "from within, out of the heart of man" (v. 21). See also the admonitions to this same effect in Matt. 7:17–20; 12:33–37; Luke 6:43–44; James 3:8–12; and Paul's list of the "works of the flesh" in Gal. 5:19–21.

HOMILETICAL INTERPRETATION

First Lesson: Deut. 4:1–2, (3–5), 6–8. How is faithfulness engendered and encouraged? In last Sunday's First Lesson Israel's story in creedal form is rehearsed, and the challenge to faithfulness is articulated as a consequence or follow-up (Pentecost 14, Joshua 24); in the Gospels from John 6 Jesus is set forth as the embodiment and fulfillment of that same story, and the challenge to faith is articulated (Pentecost 14, John 6: 60–69). The same procedure is at work here in Deuteronomy 4, but with one distinctive difference: in Joshua and John we meet a very "lively" God; in Deuteronomy we meet "statutes," "ordinances," and "commandments." (Note how in today's Gospel, Mark 7:1 ff., we also meet "the tradition of the elders.")

Faithfulness is engendered by teaching, and in order to teach ("hand on") a tradition of faith it must be codified in some way. The danger is that the focus will inadvertently shift from the God to whom the tradition witnesses to the codification, and obedience will follow this subtle shift. It is not surprising then to hear people say, "I live rightly; why did this happen to me?"

We need therefore to ask continuously: Faithfulness to what? To codes, formulaic creeds, statutes, and ordinances—or to the God out of whose involvements with us these codifications have arisen and to which they witness? Perhaps the two words, "faithfulness" and "obedience," will point the way toward making the distinction. "Obedience" will become anxious and exceedingly meticulous about "You shall not add to the word which I command you, nor take from it" (note again today's Gospel); while "faithfulness" will attune itself to the holiness and mercy of God, and the vitality of relationship with him.

Thus in vv. 9 ff. the text makes the important injunction: "Do not forget . . . but remember . . . how you stood before the Lord at Horeb . . ." Remember the story! The "statutes and ordinances" are *reminders*, and this is singularly significant. They remind, recall, re-present the

shaping events of God's encounters with his people, and of the consequences and implications of those encounters, all the way from Abraham
to Pentecost and beyond!

Second Lesson: James 1:17–27. The Epistle of James, from which
the Second Lessons for this and the following three Sundays are drawn,
has, since Luther's day, been suspect in Protestant circles for its seeming
confusion on the faith-works issue. However that may be, James is an
"activist," for whom religion can never be divorced from daily conduct.
In a day when such slogans as "It doesn't matter what you believe so
long as you are sincere" get translated into "It doesn't matter what you do
so long as it is your thing," we need very much to hear James who sees
as disastrous any divorce between faith and works, religion and life,
words and actions.

James is very conscious of the grace of God: God gives every gift, and
his giving is good; he brings new life to birth not out of coercion but "of
his own will," freely, voluntarily; he is unchangeable and invariable in
his being and giving; he grants us to be a first fruits of a vast harvest; he
has implanted a saving word. But how credible are such affirmations
today? Can we believe them? If James' readers could be reassured that
the stars were controlled by the "Father of lights," does that control
extend to man-made satellites? If what he calls "gifts" have become
fought-over human *rights,* is God as "giver" still credible? If the world
is over-populated, is "first fruits" a bad joke? And if words spill out in
cacophanous din, however are we to hear, much less do, *the* word? How
can we make James' celebration of grace credible again to ourselves and
others?

James points to fundamentals. "Be quick to hear, slow to speak, slow
to anger" so as not to obstruct the righteousness of God. We usually
respond to anger with anger; instead we need to be "quick to hear" what
is behind the anger, for it is often the shout that says, "You're not hearing
me!" By speaking too soon, the cry for understanding is silenced and
justice—rightness—is circumvented. Injustice can continue, squelching
any hesitant shoots of reconciliation and new life.

"Be doers of the word and not hearers only." One person against the
kind of world we have described is overwhelmed. But if the whole community of faith stands together, "doing the word," then revolutions may
happen. A whole community reflecting the perfect law of liberty is a
force to be reckoned with. It can be the mirror held up to society which
exposes evil and wickedness in high and low places; it can be a loud
word of truth uttered in the face of distorted and emasculated words;
it can be the sign of a new humanity over against inhumanity. There is
a challenge to the church!

Gospel: Mark 7:1–8, 14–15, 21–23. Legalism is what we call an ob-
sessive and rigid attention paid to observance of law. Its potential roots

lie in worthy concerns, namely, to be fair (no exemptions from the requirements of law), and to be respectful of law. It comes to full flower when, in the name of respect for law, the principles of fairness which have been established take precedence over the persons involved. Israel's law was an eminently "fair" expression of God's relationship with his people; it was "people oriented"; it was right (righteous), appropriate. But somehow we always manage to shift the focus. Perhaps it is because "God" or "justice" or "righteousness" are so intangible that we focus on the concrete thing: the law, the codes, the body of legislation. We become "code oriented," and before we know it we are legalists. The results would be comical were they not so tragic. The very effort to "protect" the law—to give it proper respect and honor—results in the establishment of numerous "bylaws" (the "tradition of the elders") which in the end not only nullify the law but bury people under "red tape," thus defeating the purpose of being fair. The laudable attempt fully to obey the law deteriorates into manipulation of the law (do we not search for loopholes in tax laws, for example?) in order to gain control of it and so escape it! There is nothing quite so revealing of our sinfulness as our encounters with law!

In the final analysis, legalism—whether practiced with the ten commandments, ritual, the Bible, theology, societal values, or universal principles, etc.—is an attempt to control God and the neighbor. The legalist, of course, is not aware of this, and it is always a great shock to realize that his zeal for fairness and for respect of law has in fact thwarted the just intent of law, and enabled him to escape responsive love to the neighbor. For it is not a question of whether or not to have law—we need it!—but of how we use the law we have. To paraphrase a saying of Jesus: "Law is made for man, not man for the law."

The saying of v. 15 is one of the most revolutionary statements in the NT. Jews in Maccabean and other times had suffered and died to uphold their dietary laws; Christians in many ages have suffered and died to uphold specific doctrinal interpretations and theories about the Bible. They all will have their reward; yet Jesus breathtakingly sweeps away everything that impedes the direct relationship to God. The only absolute is God. We ought not invest with divinity that which points to, represents, witnesses to God.

The Sixteenth Sunday after Pentecost

Lutheran	Roman Catholic	Episcopal	Pres./UCC/Chr.	Methodist/COCU
Isa. 35:4–7a	Isa. 35:4–7a	Isa. 35:4–7a	Isa. 35:4–7a	Isa. 35:4–7a
James 2:1–5	James 2:1–5	James 2:1–5	James 2:1–5	James 2:1–5
Mark 7:31–37	Mark 7:31–37	Mark 7:31–37	Mark 7:31–37	Mark 7:31–37

EXEGESIS

First Lesson: Isa. 35:4–7a. Interpreters usually place Isaiah 35 either in the late exilic period, in connection with Isaiah 40–55 ("Second Isaiah"), or in the early post-exilic years, along with chaps. 33–34. Thematically, chap. 35 relates closely to Isaiah 40. Both look forward to the joyful return of the exiles through a supernaturally transformed wilderness to Zion (cf. also Isa. 55:12-13).

The chapter begins with a proclamation that the wilderness through which the exiles are to pass itself will "rejoice and blossom," manifesting the glory and majesty of the verdant mountains, Lebanon, Carmel, and Sharon, indeed, the glory and majesty of God himself (vv. 1–2). There will be a safe highway through this wilderness, over which "the ransomed of the Lord shall return" (vv. 8-10; cf. 40:3-5). "Say to those who are of a fearful heart, 'Be strong, fear not!'" (v. 4). "Fear not!" is one of the great, recurring Isaianic assurances: God is in control of history and will bring about the promised redemption of his people. The assurances to this effect here correspond to a related Isaianic theme: "A remnant shall return." This declares both God's judgment—only a remnant shall return —and his steadfast love for his people, and thus the basis of their hope for the future: a remnant *shall* return. Here the prophet goes on, God will come with vengeance and recompense (cf. 34:8; 40:10). "Vengeance" may refer to the fate in store for those nations that have oppressed the Jewish people, as in the various prophetic oracles against foreign nations (e.g., Isaiah 34). Or, it may refer to the punishment which God's people must complete before they are redeemed, God's action seen as both "smiting and healing" (Isa. 19:22; cf. Hosea 1-2; Isaiah 10-12). In Isa. 40:1-2, the prophet announces that the people have now completed their punishment.

"He will come and save you." This is the gospel of the OT: God will not only deliver his people from their present oppression, but also bring about a new, transformed and everlasting era of peace for the whole creation (cf. Isa. 2, 9, 11). The verb "to save" *(yasha)* is probably represented in such significant biblical names as Hosea, Isaiah, and Joshua (Greek: Jesus), and is familiar in the transliterated cry for deliverance, "Hosanna!" Salvation means not only the ultimate condition of "everlasting joy" (v. 10), but restoration of the blind, deaf, lame, and dumb to the full use and enjoyment of their faculties while still in the wilderness, both as a foretaste and anticipatory celebration of the ultimate salvation to come, and to ease the difficulties of their remaining journey through the wilderness (cf. 40:29-31; Luke 4:18). For this latter purpose also, in an unusual fourfold poetic statement, the exiles are promised that waters/ streams/pools/springs will break forth or come to be in the wilderness/ desert/burning sand/thirsty ground (vv. 6b-7a).

Second Lesson: James 2:1-5. James often addresses his readers as "my brethren." In this lesson he urges, in effect, that in Christ there is neither "rich nor poor." Thus, he argues against partiality and discrimination within the assembly (lit., synagogue) in favor of the rich or against the poor. Possibly the christological title, "Lord of Glory" (v. 1), contains an implicit reproach against the pretensions to glory of the rich. In any event, the members of the assembly are not to show deference to the rich (politely seating the man "in splendid clothes") or humiliate the poor (ordering him to stand or sit in an inferior place, lit., "under the footstool"). Such discrimination has no place in the churches. Those who so discriminate against each other become judges with evil, inward questionings (v. 4). We might see here a call for unity in the faith (v. 1) and in the churches, as in 1 Corinthians and Ephesians. Paul had admonished the Corinthians not to humiliate those who had nothing (1 Cor. 11:22).

Something else, however, seems to be said in v. 5: that it is the "poor of the world" whom God has chosen to be "rich in faith" and heirs of the kingdom. This is also the apparent meaning of James 2:6-7 and 5:1-6: Because of their unrighteousness, the rich are to be condemned. Several of Jesus' sayings in the Gospels are to the same effect, e.g., Mark 10:17-31; Luke 6:24-25; 16:19-31 [see below, Pentecost 19, Second Lesson]. But in James 2:1-5 the author is not arguing against the rich, but against invidious treatment of the poor. What he has to say in v. 5 is a further reason for paying proper respect to the poor man who comes into the church. Such persons are rich in faith (cf. Mark 10:29-30). Moreover, they are heirs to the kingdom of God. Such also was the reported understanding of Jesus himself: Luke 6:20-21 (cf. Matt. 5:3-10); 12:33; 16:9; 20-22, 25. Other sayings of Jesus and statements of Paul indicate that it is the righteous, those who do the will of God, who will inherit the kingdom of God (e.g., Matt. 7:21; 13:43; 25:34-39; 1 Cor. 6:9). Perhaps it was generally understood that those who chose to seek the kingdom and serve God in love of neighbor would give up their possessions (Matt. 6:24 = Luke 16:13; Mark 10:21-25; cf. Luke 16:19-31).

James himself argues that discrimination against the poor man is in violation of the "royal law" of love, since it fails to meet the test, "You shall love your neighbor as yourself" (2:8-9). This suggests, incidentally, that James understood that the churches to which he wrote, if not wealthy, were for the most part composed of persons more affluent than the "poor man in shabby clothing." But each person is of equal worth: to humiliate or dishonor the poor man (2:6a) is against the law of love.

Gospel: Mark 7:31–37. In Mark 7:24–30, Jesus had extended his travels into Gentile territory, and there exorcised the demon who was troubling the Syro-phoenician woman's daughter. Now he returns, circuitously, "through the region of the Decapolis" (an extensive area in northern Palestine and east of the Jordan comprising ten Greek cities), to Galilee. As is common in Mark, the conjunction "and" *(kai)* stands at the beginning of every verse in the passage, tying the action together, and suggesting urgency or speed.

A man who was both deaf and had a speech impediment *(mogilalos)* is brought to Jesus to be healed. Healing is mediated by Jesus' touching the man's ears and tongue. Jesus looks to heaven, prays (cf. 6:41; Matt. 6:9), sighs (in compassion or as part of the treatment), and says, "Ephphatha," meaning (in Aramaic), "Be opened." The man's ears were "opened," "the bond of his tongue" was loosed, "and he spoke plainly" or "correctly" *(orthōs,* v. 35).

The story very probably was understood by Mark to fulfill the prophecy given in Isa. 35:5–6:

Then the eyes of the blind shall be opened,
    and the ears of the deaf unstopped;
then shall the lame man leap like a hart,
    and the tongue of the dumb *(mogilalos,* LXX) sing for joy.

Elsewhere Mark reports Jesus' healing the blind (8:22–26; 10:46–52) and a paralytic (2:3–12). Probably Mark saw these episodes as evidence for the long-awaited time of salvation, whether preliminary and preparatory to the coming of the kingdom of God, or somehow marking its presence. In any case, these actions bring salvation (wholeness) to those who are freed from their afflicting demons or healed.

Neither Mark nor any of the other synoptic evangelists designates such cures as "signs" or "miracles." Though there are no Jewish traditions to the effect that the Messiah would heal, it is shortly after Jesus' healing of the blind man of Bethsaida that Peter makes the startling announcement that Jesus is "the Christ" (8:22–29).

V. 36 introduces the highly problematic question of the "messianic secret." Jesus tells those who witness this healing "to tell no one"—that he is the Messiah (cf. 8:29–30), or about the healing (cf. 1:44)? The actual cure was performed privately (7:33). But, as elsewhere, the warning is to no avail: "The more he charged them, the more zealously they proclaimed it" (7:36b; cf. 1:28, 45). However, though the witnesses to the healing are impressed (v. 37; cf. 1:27; 2:12b), they apparently do not infer that Jesus is the Messiah or that the prophesied era of salvation has begun or come near.

HOMILETICAL INTERPRETATION

First Lesson: Isa. 35:4–7a. The background against which the prophet speaks is exile (specifically, the Babylonian Exile, cf. exegesis). The twentieth century has, in all probability, known more exiles and refugees than any other period of history. Countless people in congregations across our continent have grim memories of exile; many more across the face of the earth are in the midst of the harsh experience. But twentieth century man, wherever he is, feels he is a refugee. Our world—even if not upset by war—has become an alien place, from which the God of our ancestors has seemingly withdrawn, or in which he has grown dim and increasingly impotent. The call, "Fear not!" seems unforgivably naive; the invitation to hope, "He will come and save you!" sounds incredible. Yet we *want* to hope . . . and we *must* hope or go to ruin.

The experience of exile—a mix of loss, suffering, pain, doubt, anger, despair, depression, unfaith, guilt, fear, defiance, hope, grief—shatters everything the person holds dear, shatters the meanings with which he has invested his life, shatters the "story" he has thus far told. Thus the exile shattered Israel's faith, her theology, her concept of God, her self-understanding, her destiny. Could her faith-story be resurrected? The prophet, significantly, uses her old story to interpret this disastrous exile experience: He announces a "new" Passover ("He will come and save you"), a "new" covenant ("*Your* God will come"), a "new" wilderness trek (vv. 6–7), a "new" wholeness (vv. 5–6). What God did he will do. In short, the God of judgment and mercy works judgment in order to show his mercy; his judgment *is* merciful because his purpose is to save.

The way of God's working in the world comes clear in Jesus: life is attained through death because God is present in the dying to give life. So we exiles shall look for signs of life not from some ethereal realm remote from us, but precisely in the realm where we are: waters in the *wilderness,* streams in the *desert,* pools in the *burning sand,* springs in the *thirsty ground;* or, to change the figure: rays of light when we wander blindly, the redeeming word penetrating deafness, invigoration of feebleness, songs of joy where mute despair reigned.

Salvation is perceivable in these unexpected places—precisely there where all hope seems absent and irretrievable. It is the message Jesus announced: The kingdom of God is breaking in; blessed are those who, with eyes of faith, look to see it.

Second Lesson: James 2:1–5. The temptation to prefer and defer to the rich is an almost irresistible temptation. There are many reasons for it: fear, desire for gain, status, protection, power, influence. Cinderella winning the prince, and thus triumphing over not only her wretched circumstances but also her own oppressive family, is a powerful motif in any society. On the other hand, however, we equally rejoice when the "apple-polisher" is exposed and humiliated—as when Haman was hanged on the very gallows he had had made for Mordecai (the Book of Esther). There is thus an ambivalence in us over against the rich person: we feel impelled to honor him, and yet realize that in so doing we dishonor ourselves and lose our integrity and freedom. There is no feeling quite so devastating as the feeling of having "sold out" to financial interests; perhaps that is why the rich person in the world's stories is so often portrayed as a Scrooge. We *know* we can be bought, and we hate ourselves and the buyer the more!

The church in ancient times was the first to break social and class distinctions; it was revolutionary for a master to receive communion from the hand of his slave. Little wonder James speaks so passionately against showing partiality. He knew, as we are inclined to forget, that partiality is above all destructive. It destroys the "faith of our Lord Jesus Christ" in that it engenders and expresses a divided allegiance to God and Mammon. It destroys human relations because it permits a double standard. It destroys people themselves in that it nullifies the "law of love" by diametrically opposing God's purposes of compassion and salvation.

There is a wealth of sardonic irony in James' plea. The rich oppress the poor—how strange then to give the oppressor special honor! It seems singularly masochistic. But more: Stranger still that those who follow the Lord Jesus—he who had no place to lay his head—should bow down to gold rings and fine clothing. As that shaft of irony begins to penetrate our affluent mentality, we may well begin to feel uncomfortable in our comfortable pews. Where is the prophetic word and the prophetic action coming from today? Has the church willingly entered another "Babylonian captivity"?

For behold: God chose the poor in the eyes of the world to be rich in faith and heirs of the promised kingdom. No, poverty *per se* is not a ticket to the kingdom. Rather, the kingdom is at least this: *Justice;* and if God is to be fair (impartial!) to *every* person, then "the least of these my brothers" becomes the norm: the shabby man, the man who has nowhere to lay his head. In the days of the early church he had no one to champion him except the church; who is his champion today?

Gospel: Mark 7:31–37. It is a commonplace to reach to past events (or experiences or formulations) in order to interpret a present event. In such a process of reflection the past and present events illuminate and fulfill ("fill full") each other. After having caught a glimpse of a person's past we frequently exclaim, "Aha! Now I know why he did (or said) what he did." Similarly, the NT church, as it strove to fathom and communicate the meaning and effect of Jesus, constantly reached back into the OT. In that process they not only discovered the meaning of Jesus, but came to understand the depth of meaning of the OT reference. Two such "reachings back" may be noted in this pericope.

The one is the reference to Isaiah 35 (see the First Lesson) with its
glowing visions of God visiting and redeeming his people; the other is
the reference to the creation story where an unresponsive and mute chaos
is tamed and opened to light and creativity by the power of God's utter-
ance ("He has done all things well," cf. Gen. 1:31). Jesus, therefore, is
God present to save, loosing the bonds of oppression *(desmos,* bond,
fetter, v. 35; cf. Luke 13:16); his effect is re-creation. Conversely, where
there is deliverance and the creation of life, there we shall be "open" to
God's presence and ready to sing his praise.

Most of the time our faith works only in retrospect. It is only when we
look back that we are "opened," becoming aware of a providential guidance, or of the re-creative power of a harrowing experience, or of the
shaping force of an influential word. It is not too late then to speak the
word of praise and recognition—but we do feel remorse at being so slow
of heart that we had not done so earlier.

But perhaps it is just this slow and agonizing process that must be
lived through for opening and loosing to happen: To be "taken aside
from the multitude, privately," and thus experience the full bewilder-
ment of our deafness and muteness and the horrifying reality of our isola-
tion. It is there, when we "hit bottom," that we may finally *hear,* and
finally find fumbling words: "I was on the road to dissolution, but now
I may begin again. Praise God!" There faith is created again.

Can this faith also be directed forward? One of Jesus' arguments with
the leaders of the people is, in effect, "If you knew what Moses and the
prophets were all about, you would know what I am all about." So Mark
is saying in his pericope, "If you know what Isaiah (35) was saying, you
will know what is going on here." The past interprets the present and
points us toward the future. Our faith can do that too as it is nourished
by the past traditions of faith and boldly sings praises into the present
oppressions and future darknesses.

The Seventeenth Sunday after Pentecost

Lutheran	Roman Catholic	Episcopal	Pres./UCC/Chr.	Methodist/COCU
Isa. 50:4–10	Isa. 50:5–9a	Isa: 50:5–9a	Isa. 50:4–9	Isa. 50:4–10
James 2:14–18	James 2:14–18	James 2:14–18	James 2:14–18	James 2:14–18
Mark 8:27–35	Mark 8:27–35	Mark 8:27–38	Mark 8:27–35	Mark 8:27–38

EXEGESIS

First Lesson: Isa. 50:4–10. Isaiah 40–55, and sometimes 34–35, are
commonly attributed to an anonymous prophet, Second Isaiah, who lived,

perhaps among the Babylonian exiles, shortly before the end of the exile, ca. 540 BC. Isaiah of Jerusalem (c. 760-690 BC) was the first and greatest of a series of Southern or Judahite prophets. Second Isaiah may have been a fourth or fifth generation follower in this school.

Vv. 4–11 are sometimes designated "the third servant song," the others being Isa. 42:1–4; 49:1–6; and 52:13–53:12. Each refers to "the servant" of the Lord, and in the last two, interest is focused upon the past suffering or persecution of this servant and his hoped-for vindication. Who is the servant? In 42:1–4, the servant seems to be the Persian emperor, Cyrus (cf. 45:1). Elsewhere in Isaiah 40–48, however, the servant probably represents Jacob (= Israel) or the exiles. But in 49–55, the servant appears more as a single individual, perhaps the prophet himself. In 50:4–9, the writer evidently speaks of his own experience. Like other prophets, he attributes to God's inspiration the message given him to proclaim: God "wakens" his ear "morning by morning" (50:4; cf. Jer. 1:9). His task is to "sustain with a word him that is weary": presumably the tired and discouraged exiles. In vv. 5b–7, he reports the abuse to which he has been subjected because of his prophetic proclamation, and his persistence, through God's help, despite it (cf. Jer. 1:18; 15:20). Other prophets before him also had been persecuted by those who preferred to hear them prophesy "peace," "smooth things," and illusions. When the prophets would not oblige, such people regarded them as conspirators or enemies and treated them accordingly. See, e.g., Amos 7:10–12; Matt. 23:37.

Since Second Isaiah proclaims mainly the good news of coming deliverance, it is surprising that people would have taken offense. Possibly some of the exiles resented his message of coming salvation for the Gentiles (42:6; 49:5–6; cf. Jonah 4:2). Or perhaps they preferred to pity themselves (Psalm 137). Or, as some of the ancient Israelites preferred the comforts of Egypt to the hazards of the wilderness, perhaps some of the exiles did not care for Isaiah's summons to go forth (48:20).

Like Jeremiah, this Isaianic prophet looks to God for vindication and the condemnation of his oppressors (50:7–9, 11; Jer. 11:20; 17:18; 18:19–23). Like the psalmists, Second Isaiah expresses profound confidence in God's righteousness and power to make things right for those who trust in him. Vv. 10–11 probably are sardonic: The prophet is "unenlightened"—in the eyes of those who do not fear the Lord. They do not obey the voice of his servant, the prophet, but walk by their own lights. In turn, they will have to endure torment, "from my [God's own] hand" (cf. v. 9b).

Second Lesson: James 2:14–18. Luther's contemptuous characterization of James as "that straw epistle" derived mainly from his reaction to the discussion of faith and works in 2:14–26. Luther's attitude, very likely, was colored by his rejection of Catholic excesses, notably the sale of indulgences (later repudiated at Trent), and by his confusing works of the Jewish law with works of love in response to God and neighbor.

James was arguing against a kind of piety which claimed that faith or belief *(pistis)* was all that mattered. Proponents of such piety dispensed cheap spiritual blessings—"Go in peace, be warmed and filled"—as an excuse for failing to respond with needed help that might cost them something. James rightly rejects such faith as "dead" (2:17). John, Paul and Jesus would not have disagreed. "But if any one has the world's goods and sees his brother in need, yet closes his heart against him, how does God's love abide in him? Little children, let us not love in word or speech, but in deed *(en ergō)* and in truth" (1 John 3:17-18). For Paul, grace and faith were fundamental. Yet he could write, "If I have all faith, so as to remove mountains, but have not love, I am nothing" (1 Cor. 13:2b). Love is the greatest spiritual gift. Genuine faith "works" *(energoumenē)* through love (Gal. 5:6). It is not enough to say "Lord, Lord," or recite the Apostles' Creed, as Karl Barth put it, commenting on Jesus' saying at Matt. 7:21, Luke 6:46.

"If a brother or sister is naked *(gumnoi)* . . ." (v. 15): The translation "ill-clad" is possible, but weakens the point. It is not a question of fashion, but of being cold (v. 16). The same term is used in the great judgment scene in Matthew 25, translated simply as "naked." In both James 2 and Matthew 25 it is a question of responding to those in need, or failing to do so. In Matt. 25:44 those who have ignored their hungry, thirsty, lonely, naked, sick, and imprisoned neighbors address the Judge devoutly as "Lord" (cf. Matt. 7:21). But such piety will not save them.

"Go in peace, be warmed and filled . . ." (v. 16): The hypothetical Christian who pronounces this "blessing" is eager for the needy persons to *go;* "in peace" hints that they had best do so before the authorities are sent for. In any case, it is left to God, someone else, or the cold and hungry themselves to provide for their needs. "What does it profit?", literally, "What help *(ophelos)* is it?" None, to those who need help. Or the meaning may be as in 2:14: What is the advantage to the man who claims to have such faith? Clearly, conduct matters: cf. Mark 8:36; Luke 6:33-35; Rom. 2:13; 1 Cor. 3:14; Gal. 6:7-9.

A hypothetical respondent argues, in effect: There is a variety of gifts; some have faith, others have works (v. 18). James refutes this disjunction as invalid: Faith, if it is real, is expressed in what the believer does. It is to be professed with our lips *and* shown forth in our lives.

Gospel: Mark 8:27–38. We have here three major units of tradition: Peter's "confession" that Jesus is the Messiah (vv. 27–30), Jesus' first "passion pronouncement" and Peter's response (vv. 31–33), and a group of sayings about self-denial and following Jesus.

On the way to Caesarea Philippi, Jesus asks his disciples who people say he is. To the reader, familiar with the NT witness to Jesus as the

Christ, it may seem an odd question. But Jesus had not proclaimed himself Messiah or Christ. The disciples did not yet realize who he was; cf. Mark 4:41. Peter announces a new discovery! Some people thought he was John the Baptist (8:28). Others said Elijah, the great preacher of repentance who was expected to come "first" (Mark 9:11-12). Others said he was one of the (other) prophets; they, like Jesus, had proclaimed coming judgment and salvation. Jesus does not acknowledge Peter's confession, but charges the disciples to say nothing "about him," in effect, to keep his identity as Messiah a secret. Some interpreters propose that this is what Jesus himself intended (Schweitzer). Others attribute the "messianic secret" to the editorial hand of Mark (Wrede).

Jesus then teaches the disciples that the Son of man must suffer, be killed, and rise from the dead (v. 31). "And he said this plainly" (8:32a), lest there be any doubt. Peter, however, rebukes Jesus, apparently finding the prospect of his suffering and death intolerable. But then Jesus rebukes Peter, and actually identifies him with Satan! What God has ordained, and what Jesus has taught, is what must happen.

Jesus then calls the multitude, and summons any who would "come after" him, to deny himself, take up his cross and follow (8:34). Elsewhere, Jesus called on those who sought the kingdom to renounce all and follow him (e.g., Mark 10:21; Matt. 8:19-22; Luke 9:57-62; 12:33-34; 14:16-33). "Take up his cross" may be a later Christian revision if cross *(stauros)* has come to replace "staff" *(hrabdos,* Mark 6:8). Whoever would try to preserve his life in this world by keeping his own goods for himself or otherwise "playing it safe" will lose it; those who give up all else for the sake of life in the kingdom of God will save it. What does it profit *(ōphelei)* if a man gains the world, but loses eternal life, the greatest of all treasures (vv. 36-37, cf. Matt. 13:44-46)? Emphasis here is less on responding to others (cf. James 2:14-16) than upon self-denial. But unless one is willing to deny self, one will not be able to respond to others. Jesus and his words are the messenger and message to "this generation." Soon the Son of man (= Jesus, himself?) will come to judge each one according to the measure of his response to Jesus and his words (v. 38.)

HOMILETICAL INTERPRETATION

First Lesson: Isa. 50:4-10. The exegesis raises the fascinating question of why good news should cause offense. It obviously still does. In any "exilic" situation, which is filled with individual and national disillusionment, good news is received with suspicion and incredulity, and the bearers of good news are looked upon either as interesting lunatics or as dangerous radicals.

Whatever theories we may have about the identity of the "Servant" in Deutero-Isaiah, eventually we must say that the Servant represents the faithful in all times and places, whether these happen to be one or many.

God does not at any time leave himself without a witness, or, to turn that around, a witness is always embodied somewhere—even, let us remember, in a Cyrus! We must say, then, that the church is also this Servant . . . and then we must ask about her faithfulness, and how she is being regarded by the world.

What is the nature of the Servant-church's task? On the one hand it is to be a servant like Moses, that is, to stand in the gap between the people and Yahweh, bringing them "home." On the other hand it is to be like the ultimate Servant, Jesus, who is the incarnation of God's own redeeming servanthood (note that Isa. 50:4-9 is also the First Lesson for the Sunday of the Passion in Series A). While Isa. 42:1-7 gives a summary of the task in cogent breadth, and Isa. 52:13 ff. plumbs its redemptive depths, this "song" describes the task as being "the servant of the word."

Like the Isaianic Servant, the faithful community is entrusted with the word. This is no frozen, timeless word; it is not a word calcified in scroll or book. It is given "morning by morning" to the receptive ear. It is never a possession, but always a gift to those who are teachable. And the word is God's justice and mercy (cf. Isa. 42:1-7), it is God's way of working in the world. The Servant-church listens for that word, and embodies it, for the word can have reality and visibility only in a *people*.

Small wonder this word offends! Being heard afresh morning by morning it is always timely and thus disconcerting; being just it hurts, yet in the hurt is its healing. Small wonder the church's adversaries insult and shame and accuse—for the faithful community is always writing a different history than the world writes.

But beware the martyr-complex as well as the elemental pride or pretension to embodying *all* truth and virtue! The very determined and at times defiant faith that "the Lord God helps me; who will declare me guilty?" can calcify the word of the living God, and then he must seek embodiment elsewhere. Better this humility: "Anyone who fears the Lord, obeying the word of his servant, who (nevertheless) gropes in darkness and has no glimmer of light, let him trust in the name of the Lord" (v. 10, North).

Second Lesson: James 2:14-18. James is indeed a passionate preacher; his illustration is devastatingly to the point! He must have seen something like this happen, and the memory of it will not leave him. It is in an actual life-situation that we must see James' argument.

In any controversy, especially in passionate controversy, the positions tend to become polarized. That seems to be the situation out of which James writes: "I have faith" vs. "I have works" (v. 18). In the abstract, such polarizing seems inevitable and from the point of view of faithful theology, quite essential: James and Paul do seem to be "poles apart." In a real-life situation, however, such polarization becomes absurd and unproductive ("What does it profit . . .?" v. 14). It is immensely sobering for the "I have faith" side to realize that the naked neighbor would be much better off with the "I have works" side; it is equally sobering for the "I have works" side to realize that the naked neighbor has become nothing more than a peg on which to hang one more good work (cf. v. 18). Polarities profit neither the needy neighbor (v. 14) nor the Christian (v. 16).

James, who likely knew the way of "works righteousness" very well, perhaps was also particularly sensitive to a subtle and yet devastating perversion taking place, namely, fideism. He points out that the demons too "believe," in surface fashion, but they at least have the decency to shudder (v. 19). The proponents of "faith alone" are always in danger of falling back into the very morass from which Christ has rescued them; inadvertently they make faith into a justifying work. It is easily done. For the Christian whom Christ has freed from the tyranny of works righteousness, "faith alone" is a doxological reception of salvation as an undeserved and unearned gift from God. But when that "faith alone" becomes an admonitory "Only believe!", then faith has been subverted into a justifying work. Thereupon the trusting reliance upon God (Matt. 6:25 ff., "do not be anxious . . .") becomes a passing of the buck to God ("You do it, God"), and the exhortation to faith becomes a patronizing condescension to the needy neighbor ("God will supply all your needs. Only believe"). The miserable naked neighbor is left unassisted.

And it is, in the end, that needy neighbor whom we dare not remove from our sight. Faith and works both find reality—and corrective—in him. He is *needy*: no volume of words and well-wishes, however sincere or fervent or faith-full, will relieve his condition; action is required. And he is *neighbor*: he is not an opportunity to be used for well-doing (a good way to assuage a guilty conscience, by the way!), but a human being, a person with whom relationships are to be established; faith is required.

Gospel: Mark 8:27–35. In Mark's narrative the process of opening the disciples' eyes to the identity of Jesus is long and slow, and is depicted by him in a series of healing miracles which climax in the healing of the deaf-mute (Pentecost 16, Mark 7:31–37), and of the blind man of Bethsaida (8:22–25). It is perhaps not unimportant to note that Bethsaida was Peter's home town, and it is Peter who, with eyes finally opened, also finds his tongue released to speak plainly, "You are the Christ."

It is an exciting moment when a scientist, after much searching and experimentation, discovers the key formula which unlocks the mystery that has eluded him. It is a truly moving moment when a person, after much greater soul-searching and heartache and weary journeyings, discovers the key to the meaning of life. Too few of us press on to the ultimate meaning of life; it is always easier to make do in Egypt or Babylon; it is less fretful to settle for whatever meanings are handed us by current pundits and gurus and politicians. Better to pull down the horizons and be content with our little world and our cozy little meanings.

And yet there is always an Everest looming on the horizon, no matter how narrowly we limit it, inviting and terrifying. There is always the shattering blow, or the scent of something in the air, or an expression in the eye, that speaks of mystery: the mystery of life and death and complex humanity and spirit and the beyond.

We unashamedly (see v. 38) present Christ as the key to the mystery, as the bridge that links the here and the beyond, as the profound reality of God intertwined in our human existence and transcending it.

But how quickly we recoil! We want the mystery to be unravelled in keeping with our cozy little meanings—with our vision of what God should be and do, with our yearnings of how things should be set right, and our opinions as to how we should be vindicated. But no! The key to the mystery won't fit the locks of our treasure chests. It is a strange key, shaped cross-like. It opens the way to suffering and death—beyond which lies life. And that seems so contrary! But there it stands: "The Son of man must suffer . . . and be killed . . . and after three days rise again." Not "Messiah," the "anointed one" as kings and priests and prophets were anointed, but "Son of man" which includes these and, indeed, every mother's child past, present, and future; not only includes but represents them, in fact *is* them in all their glory and shame, power and weakness, honor and dishonor, grandeur and misery, suffering and death . . . and hope.

"And lead us not into temptation . . ." There is no royal road to life and its ultimate meaning. There is only the integrity of life itself, of its ambiguities. Suffering and death are not unfortunate misadventures we should seek to avoid, but are part and parcel of what it is to be human, to be sons of man and sons of God. By accepting this hard mystery of life— this is how we follow.

The Eighteenth Sunday after Pentecost

Lutheran	Roman Catholic	Episcopal	Pres./UCC/Chr.	Methodist/COCU
Jer. 11:18–20	Wisd. 2:17–20	Wisd. 2:1, 12–20	Jer. 11:18–20	Jer. 11:18–20
James 3:13–18	James 3:16–4:3	James 3:16–4:3	James 3:13–4:3	James 3:13–4:3
Mark 9:30–37	Mark 9:29–36	Mark 9:30–37	Mark 9:30–37	Mark 9:29–36

EXEGESIS

First Lesson: Jer. 11:18–20; Wisd. of Sol. 2:1, 12–20. Jeremiah reports more of his own personal experiences and feelings than any of the other prophets. Some earlier prophets also had their trials: Elijah fled in terror before the threats of Jezebel (see Pentecost 12, First Lesson), and Amos was ordered out of "the king's temple" (Amos 7:10–13). Here we have one of Jeremiah's several "confessions" or complaints. We learn from 11:21 that certain men of Anathoth, offended by Jeremiah's prophesying, told him to desist or they would kill him. We infer that Jeremiah has persisted and that his persecutors do seek his life. But the prophet has been warned by the Lord (v. 18), and declares as the word of the Lord that these would-be persecutors, and their sons and daughters, will themselves perish (vv. 22–23; cf. Amos 7:16–17). In fact, Jeremiah was frequently attacked for his unpopular prophecy of God's impending judgment. He was beaten (chap. 20), threatened with lynching (chap. 26), imprisoned (chap. 32), and thrown into a cistern (chap. 38). Anathoth had been his home (1:1), and 12:6 implies that even his own family was involved in the plotting against him (cf. Mark 6:4). Jeremiah survived their evil schemes, and lived to see the Babylonian conquest and at least the early months of the exilic period (chaps. 39–45). The prophets, along with the righteous of all ages, were an offense to those who perceived them as a challenge to the cruelties of their self-serving ways. (See Wisd. of Sol. 2:12, 14–20; Matt. 23:34–35 = Luke 11:49–51).

Like most of the other writings of the OT Apocrypha, the Wisdom of Solomon is retained in Roman Catholic and Greek Orthodox scripture to the present day. Chaps. 1:16–2:24 describe the philosophy and ethics of "ungodly men." Their philosophy is quite materialistic and "modern": Life is short, afterwards there is nothing, God is unreal. Their ethics follows logically: Enjoy life while it lasts, anything goes. "Let us crown ourselves with rosebuds before they wither"; "Everywhere let us leave signs of enjoyment"; "Let our might be our law of right" (vv. 8, 9b, 11a). To such folk, the righteous man is "inconvenient" (v. 12), for he reproaches those who live by oppression. "The very sight of him is a burden to us" (v. 15a). Such was Jeremiah to the men of Anathoth. The obvious solution is to lynch him and see if the God he trusts will deliver him (vv. 17–20; cf. Ps. 22:7-8; Matt. 27:39–43). "But the souls of the righteous are in the hand of God," while "the ungodly will be punished as their reasoning deserves" (Wisd. of Sol. 3:1, 10). If not in this life, then in the next, God will vindicate the righteous (3:2–9) and bring the wicked to their just condemnation (1:12–16; 3:10–19).

Second Lesson: James 3:13–4:3.

Like the wisdom writings in the OT, James contains an extended series of exhortations to right living. One admonition follows upon another, but it is not always clear where one section ends and the next begins. Our lesson could be seen either in connection with the discourse on the perils of wrongful speaking (3:3–12), or with the warnings against passions, covetousness, worldliness, pride, double-mindedness, and judging one's neighbor in 4:1–12. As frequently in the letter, James begins here with a rhetorical question.

Those who claim to be wise are advised to manifest their "works" (cf. 2:14–18) by good conduct "in the meekness *(prautēs)* of wisdom" (3:13). James distinguishes two kinds of wisdom. The one "from above" is "pure, peaceable, gentle, open to reason, full of mercy and good fruits, without doubting or insincerity *(anupokritos,* unhypocritical)" (v. 17). Those who conduct themselves thus hold to what they know, but without boasting or putting others down. Jesus had commended the meek as fit heirs to the kingdom (Matt. 5:5); and gentleness or meekness *(prautēs)* was commonly listed by Paul and later NT writers among the proper characteristics of the Christian life: e.g., Gal. 5:23; 6:1; Eph. 4:2 = Col. 3:12; 1 Pet. 3:15.)

The other kind of wisdom is not "from above" but "earthly, physical (or "natural," *psuchikos),* and demonic" (3:15). This use of *psuchikos* is found also in 1 Cor. 2:14 and Jude 19. Claimants to such wisdom, like the "spiritualists" in Paul's Corinthian church, are jealous and boastful. Ambition, rivalry, or selfishness *(eritheia)* prompts their behavior (3:14, 16; cf. Rom. 2:8; 2 Cor. 12:20; Gal. 5:20; Phil. 1:15–17; 2:3). The consequence of such wisdom is "disorder" or "confusion" *(akatastasia:* cf. 1 Cor. 14:33; 2 Cor. 12:20) and "every vile practice" (3:16). But those who make peace (cf. Matt. 5:9) sow [their wisdom] in peace, and bring forth the fruit of righteousness (3:18; cf. Phil. 1:11; Heb. 12:11). As in 1 Corinthians, where Paul urged the Corinthian spiritualists to test their gifts—including wisdom and knowledge—by love, which is helpful, edifies, and builds up the church, so here James calls on Christians who think themselves wise to act so as to promote peace, mercy, and gentleness and thus be true to the truth.

Self-centeredness is the main problem in 4:1–3 also. Wars, fightings, and killing derive from capitulation to one's passions (or pleasures, *hēdonai)* and coveting. There may be echoes of Rom. 7:23 in v. 1b, and of Matt. 7:7–11 in vv. 2b–3. To ask rightly is to ask for "good gifts," not those that feed one's pleasures.

Gospel: Mark 9:30–37. Mark here reports Jesus' second "passion pronouncement" (vv. 30–32), and follows it with an account of his response to the disciples' discussion as to who was "the greatest" (vv. 34–37).

"They went on from there and passed through Galilee" (v. 30a): Jesus' general direction is now toward Jerusalem, via trans-Jordan (10:1, 32, 46). "And he did not wish anyone to know" (v. 30b): This suggests that Jesus preferred to remain out of view, lest he be detained on his way to Jerusalem, where his death and resurrection were to be accomplished (cf. 10:33–34). "After three days he will rise" (v. 31): Textual variants read "on the third day," following, perhaps, Matt. 17:23. "But they did not understand . . . and were afraid to ask" (v. 32). Mark often points to the disciples' lack of understanding. Here they do not grasp the mystery of Jesus' coming passion (cf. 8:32). They acted later as if they were unprepared for what had happened. If Jesus anticipated his death, he might plausibly have looked also for his resurrection at the beginning of the new age (thus Schweitzer and Pannenberg).

Capernaum had been Jesus' home (Mark 2:1). He asks his disciples what they had been discussing "on the way." Their silence indicates that they are ashamed. Probably they had been speculating as to which of them would be greatest in the coming kingdom. Something of the sort is suggested at Mark 10:35 ff.: James and John merely wish to be given the seats of greatest glory next to Jesus when he is enthroned! In both places, Jesus replies, "If anyone would be first [in the coming kingdom], he must [now] be last of all and servant of all" (9:35; 10:43b–44; cf. 10:31).

"And he took a child . . ." (vv. 36–37): Perhaps Jesus intended to illustrate what it means to be a servant of *all* by taking and receiving *even* a child. Far from being idealized in those days, children, along with women, tax-collectors and "sinners," were considered at best second-class persons. Yet, Jesus says, who receives such a one, receives "me," indeed, God himself (v. 37), even, or particularly, in the case of those neighbors commonly regarded as inconsequential or strangers (see Matt. 25:31–46; Luke 10:25–37). But there are many sayings about children in the Gospels, and it may be that vv. 36–37 should be read in relation to these. Mark 9:41–42 refers, apparently, to new disciples; Matt. 18:2–4 to *becoming like* children in respect to humility as requisite for entering the kingdom (cf. John 3:3); Matt. 20:26–27 = Mark 10:43–44 = Luke 22:24–27; Matt. 23:11–12 refers to becoming a *servant;* and Mark 10:13–16 to receiving the kingdom as a child receives [it?], *or,* to receiving the kingdom as one receives a child *(hōs paidion).*

HOMILETICAL INTERPRETATION

First Lesson: Jer. 11:18–20. It is on the basis of Jeremiah's "confessions," one of which we have before us in the present pericope, that some scholars have advanced the theory that Deutero-Isaiah's "Servant" was Jeremiah himself. Certainly last Sunday's First Lesson, Isa. 50:4–10, has much in common with this "confession" of Jeremiah, and both carry the profound nuances of today's Gospel, Mark 9:30–37, the second pronouncement of the Passion in Mark.

As Peter recoiled from the first pronouncement of the Passion (last Sunday's Gospel), so too Jeremiah recoils with shock and anger that his *faithfulness* should precipitate the heinous conspiracy mounted against him by his own household. Both have run into the hard mystery of life under God.

Jeremiah reacts with shock, incredulous innocence, and anger—a constellation of emotions which we would today describe as part of the "grief process." And it would be no help at all, at this stage, to say to

Jeremiah, "Hush up, you blasphemer. You are saying things you don't mean. You are doing bad theology by crying for revenge." No. *We* would be doing bad theology by shutting his mouth like that (cf. Psalms 3, 10, 17, 28, 35, etc.). For Jeremiah, in crying for vengeance, is being faithful to the covenant which he has been bidden to proclaim (11:1–17); and if God himself is faithful to his own covenant, he will surely not permit this assault upon his covenantal messenger. Or will he? That is a staggering question which Jeremiah can only resolve by positing a new covenant (chap. 31); at this moment he is still short of that revelation, and so he must proceed with the shock and anger. For at this stage a word of comfort, "There, there, Jeremiah, everything's going to be all right," would be premature and unrealistic. It is always a temptation to protect ourselves and others from the ambiguities and harsh realities of life. We offer comfort too readily, and thereby deny the only reality the afflicted one knows at that moment, namely that he *hurts;* by denying his hurt we deny him. And unless that hurt is given and permitted its own integrity, healing and insight and revelation and new life cannot occur.

As Jeremiah must face the betrayal perpetrated upon him, so we too must face those circumstances which seem to contradict a God of love and justice. It is not enough to protest innocence: "But I was like a gentle lamb led to the slaughter. I did not know it was against me they devised schemes . . ." (v. 19). The covenanting God did not initiate the covenant under any illusions; he entered it "for better and for worse," with eyes wide open (cf. the "passion pronouncements," Mark 8:31; 9:31). His servants need to learn that too, else their commitment to God will be but a half commitment. For God *is* committed to his people—but that can be learned only to the degree that one suffers the sin of one's own people.

Second Lesson: James 3:13–18. Thematically we may connect this pericope with what James has to say about teachers and teaching (3:1 f.), or the unruliness of the tongue (3:3 ff.), or the various warnings in chap. 4, or, of course, treat it as a self-contained unit.

James' comparison of the two kinds of wisdom is clearly of a piece with ancient Wisdom literature, as is evidenced by the similarity of this lesson to Prov. 9:1–6, 13–18 (cf. Pentecost 13, above). Like the Hebrew Wisdom literature, James understands true wisdom to be a gift from God—it is "from above" (v. 17). He does not speculate about this, however; he keeps his eye firmly upon what happens when people interact with people.

Quite possibly James was not only aware of but also very sensitive to the dynamics of Jewish-Christian relations, and the unavoidable polarizations that were taking place not only between Jews and Gentiles but also within individual Jewish Christians themselves (himself included?). How does one deal with such and similar polarizations? Each side claims to have the right understanding and thus to be wise; competition begins and jealousies develop, fed by personal ambitions; positions are overstated and then need to be defended—and thus the "very devil" is raised. In the end truth is not served, because personal victories take the place of truth, and are won at the expense of truth.

Truth, like wisdom, comes "from above." It is no person's and no party's possession. No one "has" truth; all have glimpses of it. As two parties dialogue they may, hopefully, develop a larger glimpse of it, discovering in the process that they have made peace and are harvesting a new respect (righteousness) for one another, a profounder respect for truth, as well as a humility derived from the acknowledgement (with Paul) that we now see only dimly and know only in part (1 Cor. 13:12). And all that, put together, is surely wisdom!

We should note that James says, ". . . the wisdom from above is pure, peaceable, . . . without uncertainty . . ." A close study of these characteristics will reward us with criteria to test the glimpses of truth we have and gain—as well as of our methods of communal discourse! Secondly, like James we need to keep a close watch on the dynamics of our interactions and conversations; surely if they create "disorder and vile practices" neither righteousness nor peace will be sown or harvested. And that, in the end, is contrary to God's very nature and to his desires for the community of man. It is likewise contrary to him who said, "If any one would be first, he must be last of all and servant of all" (Mark 9:35, Gospel).

Gospel: Mark 9:30–37. A new element in this second pronouncement of the Passion is that "the Son of man will be delivered into the hands of men, and they will kill him" (v. 31). It is a chilling statement.

A child coming upon a picture of the crucifixion for the first time is deeply perplexed. Why was it done? And why was it done to *him?* We meet here the stubborn and terrifying reality of sin. There lies in the hands of men the power to *kill* (cf. Cain and Abel). When the newborn baby is delivered into the hands of parents and family, the baptized infant into the hands of a congregation, the child into the hands of teachers, the employee into the hands of a company, each "delivery" is always fraught with comfort and terror, hope and fear, growth and destruction, life and death. So much good and so much harm can be experienced and perpetrated, so much life can be created and so much killing can be done. The ultimate risk of being human—for the Son of man and for every son of man—is to be killed by the hands of men (cf. First Lesson).

The child (v. 36), whether that be a literal child or any vulnerable person (cf. exegesis), is the perfect example of "being delivered into the hands of men." Will he be "received" or not? The evangelist wrote poignantly of Jesus, "He came to his own home, and his own people received him not" (John 1:11). Therefore, "Whoever receives one such

child in my name receives me; and whoever receives me, receives not me
but him who sent me" (v. 37). For "receiving" is the opposite of "killing";
it is giving life instead of taking it.

But "receiving" requires the servant posture, else it is not genuine
"receiving," only condescension and patronage. For this reason the aspira-
tion to be "the greatest" (v. 34) is always potentially participation in
destruction, if only in the fact that to be greatest necessitates someone
else to be less and someone to be least.

But now the strange paradox: To be "servant of all and last of all" is
to be vulnerable; and vulnerability, given the reality of evil, is an invitation to the destructive hands of man; "they will kill him." Yet Jesus, the
ultimate servant (see Mark 10:45), expresses a confident hope: "After
three days he will rise." The church, like its Head, is called to be servant
(see above, Pentecost 17, First Lesson), and to suffer the vulnerability of
servanthood in hope of the promise of resurrection. But she should not
entertain illusions of grandeur (v. 34); rather, by "receiving" the children
of men, witness to the world that "delivery into the hands of men" is
also participation in salvation.

The Nineteenth Sunday after Pentecost

Lutheran	Roman Catholic	Episcopal	Pres./UCC/Chr.	Methodist/COCU
Num. 11:24–30	Num. 11:25–29	Num. 11:25–29	Num. 11:24–30	Num. 11:24–30
James 5:1–11	James 5:1–6	James 5:1–6	James 5:1–6	James 5:1–6
Mark 9:38–50	Mark 9:37–42, 44, 46–47	Mark 9:38–43, 45, 47–48	Mark 9:38–48	Mark 9:38–50

EXEGESIS

First Lesson: Num. 11:24–30. Here is a marvelous fragment of early
tradition describing those ancient days when Moses and the people of
Israel were still in the wilderness. The law had been given, but the people
were not yet in the Promised Land. The episode is framed by accounts
of the Israelites' complaining that they had no meat such as they had en-
joyed in the good old days in Egypt, and of the Lord's punishing them
with a surfeit of meat and a terrible plague.

In Num. 11:16–17 the Lord had instructed Moses to gather seventy
of the elders to whom he would then give some of the spirit that earlier
had been put upon Moses alone. Thus Moses would not have to "bear the
burden of the people" by himself (11:17). Moses gathered the seventy
and placed them in a circle around the tent, which was outside the

Israelites' camp. The Lord then put some of the spirit upon the seventy elders, whereupon—on that occasion only—they prophesied (vv. 24–25).

Eldad and Medad, also apparently elders, perhaps among the seventy Moses had chosen, remained in the camp, but nevertheless received the spirit and prophesied there. Joshua—who later led Israel into the land of Canaan—was indignant at this irregularity, and urged Moses to forbid their prophesying in the camp. Moses' response shows that he was not thinking of his own prerogatives, but of the wonderful gift of the spirit and prophecy: "Would that all the Lord's people were prophets, that the Lord would put his spirit upon them!" Moses' reply to Joshua foreshadows Jesus' answer to John regarding the "strange exorcist": "Do not forbid him; for he that is not against you is for you" (Luke 9:49–50; cf. Mark 9:38–40).

The location of the tent of meeting outside the camp (cf. Exod. 33:7–11 and the later Priestly concept in Num. 2:2) probably expressed God's holiness or "separateness," and the corresponding importance of the people's keeping their distance from him (cf. Exod. 19:10–24). The spirit of God was associated with prophecy from quite early times, possibly going back to ecstatic Canaanite prophetism, e.g., 1 Sam. 10:6, 10. All Israel, if not all mankind, would receive the spirit and prophesy in the "latter days," according to Joel 2:28–29. The early Christians in Jerusalem had such an experience on the day of Pentecost (Acts 2:1–21).

The account in Num. 11:24–30 is similar to the story in Exod. 18:13–27 in which Moses accepts his father-in-law's advice, and appoints judges who "will bear the burden" (18:22) of judging the innumerable disputes among the Israelites in the wilderness. In Numbers, however, it is not clear how the seventy were to assist Moses, and we hear no more of them afterwards.

Second Lesson: James 5:1–11. Our lesson has two parts: Vv. 1–6 call on the rich to bemoan the judgment in store for them. Vv. 7–11 call upon the "brethren" to be patient and steadfast, for the *parousia* of the Lord has come near (*ēngiken*).

Elsewhere James has inveighed against the rich, and declared that the poor would inherit the kingdom (2:2–7). Numerous traditions, especially in Luke, report that this had been Jesus' understanding also, e.g., Luke 6:20, 24; 12:16–21. In the Parable of the Rich Man and Lazarus (Luke 16:19–31), Lazarus was not said to have been righteous, just poor; nor the rich man wicked—other than by living in luxury while Lazarus starved at his gate—just rich. Perhaps Jesus' saying at Matt. 6:24 sums it up: "You cannot serve God and possessions" (=Luke 16:13). See also Mark 10:17–25, where Jesus called on the rich "young" man to sell all and give to the poor if he wished to have treasure in heaven. "All things are possible with God" (Mark 10:27) has been seized upon by latter-day Christians who hoped to have it both ways. But as J. Weiss observed, it would be more pious to honor Jesus' command than to hope for a miraculous dispensation (see also Luke 12:33). The early church in Jerusalem evidently did sell all, gave to the poor, themselves became poor, and awaited the fulfillment of the promise (Acts 2:43–47).

That those excluded from the kingdom of God would weep and howl (or "gnash their teeth") is often stated, especially in Matthew (also Luke 13:28). On the decay and rust of earthly treasures, see Matt. 6:19–21. Holding back the wages of laborers was one of the offenses proscribed by the ancient law (Deut. 24:14–15), while living in luxury, heedless of God's law and impending judgment had been condemned by the prophets (Amos 6:4–7; Isa. 5:8–23). It is not clear who "the righteous man" condemned and killed by the rich may have been (v. 6). Perhaps he represents all the righteous who have perished through neglect and oppression (see Wisd. of Sol. 1:16–2:20; Luke 11:49–51).

James urges the church (or churches) of his day to keep the faith, for the time of judgment and redemption is near. The image of the farmer awaiting the fruit of the earth draws upon messianic symbolism and assures the readers that this time is coming, though they still may have to wait (cf. Mark 4:26–29). James' admonition against grumbling recalls the tendency of Israel in the wilderness to complain as if doubting God's ability to bring them into the Promised Land or care for them in the meantime (Exod. 16; Num. 11). It also echoes Jesus' saying against judging (Matt. 7:1–2; cf. Rom. 2:1–3; 14:10). So near is the judgment that the Judge is already standing at the doors! (cf. Mark 13:29). But those who have kept the faith in patience and steadfastness need not be anxious, for "the Lord is compassionate and merciful."

Gospel: Mark 9:38–50. Here we have at least five different sayings collected by Mark (or an earlier "redactor") and arranged on the basis of catchwords or verbal association. Beginning in v. 37, three sayings are given, all involving reference to Jesus' "name." The first declares that one who, mindful of Jesus' name, receives a child, receives Jesus himself (cf. Matt. 25:31 ff.). The exorcist of v. 38 who uses Jesus' name is not to be stopped simply because he is not a disciple. Like Moses (Numbers 11), Jesus recognizes that God may act through other persons than those authorized by men. Strangers who do the will of God may be thought of as fellow-workers. (But cf. Matt. 12:30; Acts 19:13 f.) A third saying referring to Jesus' name follows in v. 41: Those who do even a minor service to Jesus' followers will have their recompense. This saying may reflect the later question of hospitality to Christian missionaries: cf. 3 John 5–8; Luke 10:7–8.

The "little ones" who believe in Jesus (v. 42) seem to be Jesus' followers, perhaps new converts, rather than believers who are children (cf. Matt. 10:42). Paul expresses similar concern lest supposedly more mature Christians cause new converts to "stumble" (1 Cor. 8:7–13).

The longer saying, vv. 43–48, is linked to the foregoing by the verb *skandalizein*, translated (RSV), "to sin," at vv. 42 and 43, and by other associations. The idea elaborated in the threefold saying about hand, foot, and eye is that eternal life is worth any sacrifice, for the alternative is eternal torment in gehenna. The saying may be offensive to many (cf. Matt. 19:12). It is the most vivid statement by Jesus in the Gospels as to the prospective fate of the condemned, even with vv. 44 and 46 omitted. But it is consistent with his other summons to repent, to choose between saving one's life in this world, or abandoning all for the hope of life in the kingdom of God. The idea of eternal torment in gehenna (v. 48) is omitted in Matthew's and Luke's versions. V. 49 may have been a separate saying (cf. Luke 12:49 f.) added to v. 48 on the basis of the catchword, "fire."

Two other sayings about salt then follow. The first, v. 50a, seems to parallel Matt. 5:13 = Luke 14:34 f., and, like numerous other sayings (e.g., at Matt. 5:14–16; 6:19–24), calls for radical obedience or choice between the life of discipleship, and the comfortable way of accomodation to the world. The final "salt" saying, in v. 50b, may correspond to the exhortation to gracious speech in Col. 4:6. It calls for mutual accord or peace, a fitting ending to the group of sayings that began with the disciples' dispute about which of them was the greatest (9:33–35).

HOMILETICAL INTERPRETATION

First Lesson: Num. 11:24–30. In Exod. 18:13 ff. we have a straightforward accounting of how Moses, acting upon his father-in-law's recommendations, appoints trustworthy "rulers" to settle day-to-day disputes. In this First Lesson, however, that narrative has become an "ordination" service, complete with a theophany and impartation of "the spirit that was upon Moses." Judging by what happens again and again in liturgical history, we may have here an example of how institutions, appointments, traditions, etc., which were born of practical concerns, in time are sacralized and divinely rationalized. Joshua's negative reaction to the two "unordained" prophesiers is therefore all the more interesting. For once an appointment or tradition has been divinely sanctioned, enormous energy is invested in maintaining "good order," "proper procedures," and "legitimate certification." Moses' wistful prayer, "Would that all the Lord's people were prophets," is a wish breathed whenever the church becomes rigid and unresponsive, or when leaders become jealous of their own power when a wider distribution of authority is proposed.

Moses' prayer is also the hint of major developments in the conception and experience of the spirit of God. Moses has the spirit; here it is shared —at least for a short time. In later eras the prophets especially are "seized by the spirit," and as the exegesis points out, Joel envisaged a general outpouring of the spirit, which the church has subsequently celebrated on Pentecost. The movement is from the few to the many; and certainly in the church today there is a new recognition and appropriation of the gift of the spirit by all God's people, independent of denominational lines. While God "is not a God of confusion but of peace" and therefore "all things should be done decently and in order" (1 Cor. 14:33, 40), this is not to be interpreted statically. The Spirit "blows where it wills" (John 3:8), and blessed is he who, like Moses, recognizes his manifestations in unexpected places and rejoices (see also the Gospel). God always breaks out of the strictures we place upon him; our anxiety about "irregular" religious beliefs and practice has left its sad trail of heresy and witch-hunts.

Coupled with this freedom of the spirit is the interesting location of the tent of meeting *outside* the camp. While this is an expression of God's holy separateness, the author of Hebrews sees as highly significant the fact that Jesus, like the ancient sin offerings which were burned outside the camp, "also suffered outside the gate" (Heb. 13:11 f.) "Therefore," he writes, "let us go forth to him outside the camp, bearing abuse for him" (Heb. 13:14). God, who is always also outside the camp, keeps beckoning us on; he is "for us" and "with us," but can also always take a stand "against us" (cf. the Second Lesson: "Behold, the Judge is standing at the doors").

Second Lesson: James 5:1–11. When the hardships, oppressions, and injustices of life strike hard, what sort of hopes do we nourish? Surely they involve at the very least some vague anticipation of better days to come. James details two ways in which the faithful community has tried to handle the evil and wickedness of life.

Vv. 1–6 of this Second Lesson reflect vividly the Jewish and early Christian apocalyptic expectations of late OT and early NT times. The "Day of the Lord" would signal God's cataclysmic intervention on behalf of his people, inaugurating the New or Messianic Age in which Israel would be vindicated and enthroned over all her enemies. Here we observe how oppression and injustice can gall to the point of violence. The anger in these verses comes from centuries of Jewish subjugation by foreigners in which faith in the eventual triumph of righteousness has well-nigh evaporated. It is the anger our age has been experiencing from minority groups, and as Martin Luther King invoked the ancient exodus images, so here James invokes the ancient "Yahweh of hosts," Yahweh the *warrior* God of Israel (cf. also Revelation). That the "rich" become the symbol of oppressive wickedness is not surprising, for the oppressed minority has little choice but to assume that the oppressors have all the wealth, since they themselves have none. A theological student working in a black ghetto had in his apartment a picture of his parents' home. Though it was a "modest bungalow," to the teen-agers it was a mansion, and they automatically expected he had bushels of money to share with them!

Their voiced and unvoiced expectations were for a great upheaval that would put "whitey" in his place. Vv. 7–11 reflect the Christian community's eschatological hopes: The Lord will come, is indeed at the door; therefore be watchful and prepared to meet him and enter his promised kingdom. Here the emphasis is on patient suffering, buoyed up by the shortness of time left and by examples of outstanding steadfastness (the prophets and Job). God here is not the warrior "God of hosts," but rather the Judge who dispenses justice, motivated by compassion and mercy for his faithful suffering ones.

The church has largely adopted this latter attitude, and has consequently been accused of quiet, other-worldly withdrawal, depending upon the Last Judgment to condemn the unrighteous. But a growing realization of the oppression and exploitation of minority groups and native peoples is forcing the church to adopt a more aggressive stance in keeping with James' castigation of the "rich." That is a painful message to a church established in an affluent society, and therefore the church must herself first hear James' strong words before she can with credibility and power attack wider patterns of oppression.

Gospel: Mark 9:38–50. This Gospel is a veritable "catch-word quilt." Here is an opportunity, however, to share some of the history of the formation of the Gospels (see exegesis and parallel passages). As well, here is an opportunity to trace the development of "hell" from the Valley of Hinnom (Hebrew, gê hinnōm), the infamous ravine where Ahaz instituted the sacrifice of children through fire to Molech (2 Chron. 28:3; 33:6; Jer. 7:31; 19:5 f.; 32:35). Josiah ended these rites (2 Kings 23:10), and the valley eventually became the perpetually smouldering dump for Jerusalem's garbage. The burning, smokey, wormy (vs. 48), unclean vale produced the imagery for the place of divine punishment (cf. Enoch 27:2; 90:26 f.; 4 Ezra 7:36).

The strange exorcist narrative recalls the First Lesson. The power of the name is an intriguing conception. The ancient notion that a demon could be exorcised by means of the name of a more powerful spirit is not so strange when we realize we still "exorcise" law-breakers "in the name of the Law," and threaten policemen "in the name of" the Chief of Police who "is our friend"! The power of a name—and not least the name of Jesus—has been used to achieve innumerable good and bad ends, and our religious divisions have been maintained "in the name of" both worthy and perverse reasons. Whatever may be said against the disciple John, he deserves praise for being jealous of the name of Jesus. He will not have that name used for nefarious enterprises. Would that we had a like concern for that name, and the names of our fellows.

The statement, "he who is not against us is for us," is a marvelous expression of tolerance; yet it seemingly contradicts another saying of

Jesus, "He who is not with me is against me" (Matt. 12:30). While the contexts of the two sayings are different, it is just that difference that can lead us into consideration of the vexing question, "When does tolerance become wishy-washiness?"

The "cup of cold water" saying raises the issue of reward. The NT speaks of rewards in the context of a merciful and caring Father who sees even the sparrow fall, and thus recognizes such small services as expressions of his own will. In light of this, causing others (v. 42) and oneself (vv. 43–48) to stumble is all the more heinous.

The "salt" sayings are difficult to understand. Salt for the ancients was a valuable preservative as well as a seasoning; in addition, salt made OT sacrifices acceptable (Lev. 2:13), thus perhaps symbolizing purity or covenantal faithfulness. Fire usually symbolized purgation, judgment, persecution. These verses thus stress the radicalness of the call to discipleship and the imminence of judgment. For God—*because* he is a caring God—is not a loosely permissive God.